THE MYSTERIES OF STONEHENGE

On an unknown day some four thousand years ago, construction began for a temple like no other built before or after. Today, Stonehenge survives in partial ruin, carrying many secrets yet to be penetrated by the mind of man—as well as lost knowledge which mortal man may never know.

Author Fernand Niel takes the reader into the Stonehenge of legend and fantasy . . . and the Stonehenge of today, which gives up its secrets reluctantly, and only to those with the persistence and the seeking urge to penetrate its past. This Fernand Niel has done, in a book which reverberates with the secrets of the Cosmos.

THE MYSTERIES OF STONEHENGE is one in a series of Avon Books dedicated to exploring the lost secrets of ancient peoples and earlier times . . . secrets which challenge mankind today—and which may hold the key to our own future.

Other books in the series:

THE MYSTERIES OF EASTER ISLAND	25189	$1.75
THE MYSTERIES OF CHARTRES CATHEDRAL	24596	$1.75

Fernand Niel

Translated
by Lowell Bair

AVON
PUBLISHERS OF BARD, CAMELOT, DISCUS, EQUINOX AND FLARE BOOKS

All the drawings, maps, and plans illustrating the book are by the author.

The photographs are by Gillette Niel, except for numbers 4, 5, 11, 13, and 15.

AVON BOOKS
A division of
The Hearst Corporation
959 Eighth Avenue
New York, New York 10019

Published by arrangement with Editions Robert Laffont, S.A.
Library of Congress Catalog Card Number: 75-21914

ISBN: 0-380-00473-9

First Avon Printing, September, 1975

Printed in the U.S.A.

CONTENTS

FIGURE 1

FOREWORD

The aim of this book is to better acquaint the public with one of the world's most mysterious monuments: the prehistoric structure of Stonehenge, about 75 miles south-southwest of London and 8 miles north of Salisbury.

It is not, of course, completely unknown to the cultivated public. Books on prehistoric subjects refer to it often, and well-illustrated articles on it have appeared in many magazines. Although it would be an exaggeration to say that pictures of its gigantic trilithons are familiar to everyone, it is nevertheless true that many people can identify them without hesitation.

I would like to stress one point at the outset: Stonehenge is not a megalithic monument that can be put in the same category as dolmens and menhirs. The stones that compose it are not in their natural state. They were shaped by its builders, sometimes with great skill. Furthermore, we find such exactness and architectural refinements in its design, and its construction reveals such great knowledge and technical accomplishments, that it stands apart from other megalithic monuments despite the precision and fine workmanship displayed by some of them, such as the covered passage of Bagneux-Saumur in the Maine-et-Loire department of France, the Antequera dolmen in Andalusia, "Brodgar's Ring" in the Orkney Islands, and the rectangular cromlech of Crucuno in the Morbihan department of France. These monuments, chosen from among many others, show unerring skill in their design, construction, or orientation, but they çannot be compared with Stonehenge even though they date from the same period, probably to within two or three centuries.

If it were transported to Carnac or Locmariaquer, in France, Stonehenge would be as out of place as at Luxor or Athens, if not more so. It is a completely exceptional monument. The prodigious interest it has aroused in Great Britain is one proof of this. But it is also known all over the world, and its great fame would be inexplicable if it were an ordinary megalithic monument like so many others in Western Europe. In 1900, a bibliography of books and articles on Stonehenge contained more than six hundred titles. By now, that figure may have doubled.

Each year nearly 200,000 visitors pay their sixpence to go inside the enclosure of Stonehenge and see it from close up. In one day I saw more than a thousand people come there, and among them I was able to identify Canadians, Germans, Dutchmen, Frenchmen, and a Japanese. Every year at sunrise on the morning of June 21, the crowd is so dense that an impressive number of guards is needed to keep order. And all this takes place without any advertising or publicity: no billboards, only simple road signs like all the others, and there is no regular means of transportation to Stonehenge, even from the nearest towns.

Not only archaeologists but also painters, poets, philosophers, historians, geologists, astronomers, engineers, and architects have been gripped by the fascination of Stonehenge, which I myself have felt. There are also theosophists, anthroposophists, radiesthesists, spiritualists, followers of neo-Druidic religions, and various kinds of visionaries. Finally, there is the general public, people of all social backgrounds: lawyers, doctors, clergymen, teachers, soldiers, and civil servants.

Is that intense interest and curiosity justified? The reader will judge for himself at the end of this book, but I believe the same is true of Stonehenge as of certain other ancient works, such as the aligned menhirs at Carnac, France, the Great Pyramid, the Zimbabwe ruins in Rhodesia, Tiahuanaco in the Andes, and the Easter Island statues: They all pose unsolved problems and seem to defy the perspicacity of modern scientists.

A great deal has been accomplished since the sixteenth century when the famous architect Inigo Jones became fascinated by Stonehenge and wrote the first-known comprehensive study of it, illustrated with admirable drawings that included an attempt to depict its original state. Many questions have been given satisfactory answers, precise plans have been drawn, intelligent and methodical excavations have been carried out, and a number of discoveries have been made, some of them sensational. Moreover, all false hypotheses on Stonehenge, sensible or not, have now been swept away, along with the absurdities spawned by foggy minds and overheated imaginations.

But important questions still remain unanswered, for one of the most bewildering aspects of that enigmatic structure is its uniqueness. Nowhere else in the world is there anything comparable to it. Stonehenge was probably a solar temple, a kind of sanctuary. It has two dominant figures: its circular shape in the horizontal plane and, vertically, the shape of its trilithons, which are composed of two upright stones joined at the top by a third stone that forms a lintel. It has a complexity that partly explains the number of articles written on various details of it, as well as the fact that books on the monument as a whole, including this one, tend to be rather long.

I have spent thirty entire days studying Stonehenge at the site itself. Among other things, I have verified its measurements and alignments. My work was facilitated by a plan on the scale of 100 to 1 and a model on the scale of 50 to 1. But although my own studies were one of the factors that prompted me to write this book, it is based to a large extent on the great works of British scientists. I have not, of course, read all the books and articles that make up the incredible bibliography of Stonehenge, but I have been able to obtain the main ones from either bookstores or libraries.

Except for a few booklets that present a popularized treatment of the subject, all those works contain technical explanations that give certain passages a scientific tone. In this connection I would like to call attention to two important points. First, pure archaeology is still unable to explain Stonehenge completely; although it has given many unquestionable answers, it has not solved all the problems, and that is why other disciplines, such as geology, astronomy, and mathematics, have been utilized. Second, we cannot discuss such a monument without referring to figures and the techniques that seem to have been used by its builders. This book does not escape from that obligation.

Most of the great works on Stonehenge contain many plans, diagrams, maps, and drawings to which the reader is often referred. This book also follows that rule. Such illustrations are absolutely necessary for giving a concrete idea of the monument. And anyone who visits it must often consult a guidebook or a plan to identify its various parts. Since Stonehenge has been partly destroyed—more than half of the stones that once composed it have disappeared—it is difficult if not impossible to form a mental reconstruction of it by oneself; on the whole, one can picture its original state more precisely by looking at drawings than by visiting the actual site.

The monument that can be seen today was built over earlier sanctuaries. All that remains of them is now below the level of the ground. They have been carefully studied by archaeologists but are covered by earth except during periods of research. Thousands of uninformed visitors do not even suspect their existence.

Important remnants of Stonehenge's past can thus be known only by learning about them from books illustrated with appropriate drawings. And without such drawings extremely revealing details might escape notice or fail to be understood. That is why I have included a large number of them in this book. I have also included photographs that, I hope, will help to make the reader better acquainted with Stonehenge and its special atmosphere.

One final point: Throughout this book the reader should always bear in mind that Stonehenge is in the westernmost part of Europe and was built in the fourteenth or fifteenth century B.C.

At that time and place, as far as we know, there were no nations, cities, or civilizations comparable to those of the eastern Mediterranean basin, to mention only the nearest ones. We know so little about the people living in the region of Stonehenge at the time when it was built that we designate them by the name of the utensil they used for drinking or by the rather vague term "the Wessex Culture," based on objects taken from their graves in Wessex. We know that they were divided into tribes, that they practiced farming and herding, that they knew bronze but still used stone tools, and that they buried their dead in circular graves. Aside from a few details of their weapons, utensils, and adornments, that is nearly all we know about them. It is not enough to differentiate them clearly from other peoples living in Western Europe at the same time.

Such is the context in which Stonehenge exists. We should never lose sight of it.

PART ONE

Stonehenge and Its Environs

Salisbury Plain

The name of Salisbury must make most Britons think of one of their country's most beautiful Gothic cathedrals and the megalithic monument of Stonehenge, two magnificent manifestations of man's religious spirit, separated by three thousand years. They are more than enough to assure the fame of Salisbury. It is a pleasant town crossed by many waterways, highly animated but not yet blemished by any excessively noisy or visible industry. It is the capital of Wiltshire, which, with Hampshire, Dorsetshire, and Berkshire, once constituted the kingdom of Wessex. It is from here that, after having admired the cathedral and its 400-foot spire, one leaves to visit Stonehenge.

The road runs north, in the direction of Marlborough, and passes the ancient fortress of Old Sarum, the Sarbiodunum of the Celts, on which four Roman roads converged. This site was the origin of modern Salisbury, also called New Sarum. Deep moats and the remains of old gray walls made of small stones are partially covered by a green lawn. Rising from a pasture is a green fortress completely covered by the grass so dear to the English, which we left at the foot of Salisbury Cathedral and will find again around the gigantic monoliths of Stonehenge. The ramparts, dotted with dark, almost

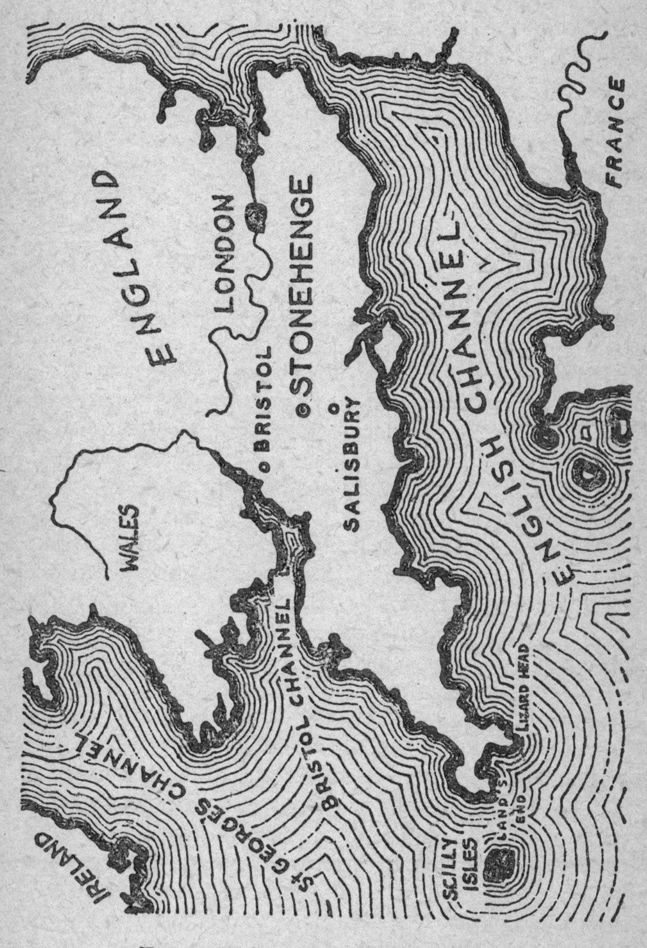

FIGURE 2—Stonehenge and its environs.

black foliage of trees that look like balls, rise in several concentric enclosures. The whole structure has the shape of a fairly regular circle. The highest part of it gives a broad view of the surrounding countryside. After Old Sarum begins what is called, probably not without humor, Salisbury Plain.

Salisbury Plain is surely the most deeply undulating of all plains. In 1634 John Evelyn spoke of its "evenness," and twelve years later Samuel Pepys saw "frightening heights" in it. Unfortunately, not many people are able to embellish things this way, in one direction or the other, and for ordinary mortals the truth lies between Evelyn's evenness and Pepys' heights. Salisbury Plain is a series of depressions and broad plateaus. Its average altitude is about 450 feet, and its highest point must be Beacon Hill, 670 feet, 12 miles from Salisbury.

The roads across that strange plain are seldom level; they form an almost uninterrupted series of rises and descents. What gives the illusion of flatness, and may explain why the region is called a plain, is that from the tops of those rounded hills the horizon seems to be at the same level in all directions. The depressions and valleys disappear, and one has the impression of being in the middle of a vast plain or on an immense, high plateau with a flat, uniform horizon.

The whole region is well cultivated despite the thinness of the soil over a layer of hard chalk. This underlying layer appears whenever the slightest hole is dug in the ground. In some places where recent digging has uncovered it, it has a beautiful white color. Fragments of that chalk are strewn over grain fields, giving them a grayish tinge in winter, when seen from a distance. Alternating with the grain fields are pastures with black and white cows and black-muzzled sheep. If it were not for the hangars of airfields and the barracks of army camps, one could imagine the horizon of Salisbury Plain as it may have been in the time of Old Sarum and even of Stonehenge. The only difference was probably that the clumps of dark green foliage were larger and more numerous.

All settlements are on the banks of streams, at the

bottoms of valleys. They therefore cannot be seen from the high points of Salisbury Plain, and without the pastures and cultivated fields the region would seem almost uninhabited. The farmhouses are widely separated and often hidden by clumps of trees. The uniformity of that monotonous landscape is broken only by the military camps of Tildworth, Bulford, Larkhill, and Tilshead.

Salisbury Plain has the shape of a triangle, its apex touching Salisbury to the south and its base extending along the Vale of Pewsey to the north. The western and eastern sides are drawn by the winding courses of two streams: the Naddern and the Bourne. The triangle is divided into two roughly equal parts by the Avon of Hampshire or Salisbury, not to be confused with the tributary of the Severn that passes through Stratford-on-Avon, Shakespeare's birthplace, or with the small coastal stream of the same name, which empties into the Bristol Channel. The Naddern, the Bourne, and the Avon have a junction at Salisbury.

Salisbury Plain has another noteworthy feature: It marks the convergence of the downs, chalky hills that run across the whole southern part of England in an east-west direction. To the north are the Berkshire Downs, to the east the North and South Downs, to the west the Mendip and Dorset Downs. Salisbury Plain is the place where the downs meet, and Stonehenge is at the center of that plain.

The first town north of Salisbury is Amesbury, 8 miles away on the Marlborough road, in the middle of Wiltshire. Amesbury is a small town built in a bend of the Avon. Its cottages with white walls and woodwork painted various colors, mostly black, red, and light blue, give a touch of brightness to the monotony of the plain. It is here, in the "holy house of Amesbury," that Queen Guinevere, wife of King Arthur, is said to have retired after abandoning her husband's court. Having found her there, he bade her farewell on the day before his last battle against the Saxons. Mourned and honored by all, Guinevere died in Amesbury Abbey. But while the town is famous for its ancient convent related to the legends of King Arthur, it is even more famous for its nearness to Stonehenge, about 2 miles away.

At Amesbury the Salisbury-Marlborough road crosses an important road coming from London and Andover. The latter runs through the town, then branches off in two directions 2 miles beyond it. The left branch goes toward Exeter and Plymouth, the right branch toward Warminster, Bath, and Bristol. The fork is at the bottom of one of those unexpected depressions that are so numerous in Salisbury Plain. Stonehenge is a few hundred yards farther on, at the edge of the road to Bristol.

First Contact

According to many British authors, one's first sight of Stonehenge produces a feeling of disappointment. There is some truth in that. When a visitor coming from Amesbury has passed a farmhouse and a wooded enclosure and suddenly sees the famous stones about half a mile away, he does not realize their actual size, especially since they do not stand out from each other. They seem to be clustered in a small space, and that gives them the appearance of a mass of natural rocks. He also seems to be looking down on them, though he is really on their level. The trouble is that he sees them from too far away. That impression is probably diminished when they are approached more rapidly, in a car, for example.

Furthermore, Stonehenge is no longer alone on Salisbury Plain. The roads leading toward it have heavy traffic that becomes infernally dense on some weekends. The cars are only a few feet apart from each other, and there are often endless military convoys composed of heavy trucks whose uproar fails to drown out the noise of supersonic airplanes. This is also a cause of disappointment since it is impossible to avoid the road. The fields alongside it are nearly all fenced in, and the frequent rains transform them into veritable bogs.

Perhaps the best way to appreciate Stonehenge in all its purity is to look at some of the paintings of it made more than fifty years ago. We then see it as we would like it to be, on a lonely moor beneath a heavy sky, a shepherd and his flock accentuating the solitude around the monument.

The road dips abruptly, and Stonehenge disappears.* When it reappears after a short rise, it is only 200 yards away. If he has not been informed of it, the visitor passes a big pointed stone without paying much attention to it. Beside it is a small, old milestone with the inscription: "LXXX miles from London." He buys his ticket and hurries through the gate in the fence around the monument. He walks across a beautiful carpet of grass. He barely notices a shallow, grass-lined ditch because he is impatient to see what is behind a peristyle composed of enormous, rather irregular stones joined in pairs by lintels.

The circular colonnade is what strikes him most when he arrives at Stonehenge. He quickly sees that it is incomplete since a large part of its circumference is missing, but enough of it remains to arrest his gaze, and that impressive part of the monument always arouses admiration. He has noticed even higher stones standing behind the colonnade, but they are only partially visible. His first impression is therefore that of a rather well preserved monument. And that impression is false.

Once he is inside, after having gone through one of the "gateways" formed by two pillars and their lintel, he finds himself in the middle of a complicated structure. A few relatively low stones and some gigantic groups, each composed of two uprights joined at the top by a lintel, may give the illusion of a certain order, but everything else forms the most complete chaos imaginable, especially on the side opposite the entrance of the monument. Blocks of stone are tilted or lying on the ground, sometimes on top of each other, half buried, whole or broken in two or three pieces, all of which gives the impression that Stonehenge has suffered from the effects of an earthquake and not a deliberate destruction by man. Did the wrath of the gods descend

*Since this paragraph was written, that deep depression has been leveled.

on the temple in the form of an earthquake? One might think so, and in my opinion that spectacle is partly responsible for the feeling of disappointment mentioned by British authors. The monument is approached from its best-preserved side, but behind that deceptive façade lie ruin and disorder.*

There are also the drawbacks associated with all famous places. The parking lot is often too small to contain the vehicles of all kinds that bring a steady stream of visitors. It sometimes seems that the whole population of a county is passing through: young and old couples, newlyweds holding hands, bearded artists, groups of friends, clergymen, young women in gaudy clothes (a sky-blue blouse with orange pants, for example), schoolboys in green jackets and caps, lovers indifferent to the giant monoliths, old ladies in pink or lavender hats, boarding-school girls wearing straw hats surrounded by wide red ribbons and set squarely on their heads, military men grouped according to their services (artillery, infantry, air force), tourists clustered around their discoursing guides, and, above all, whole families, including grandparents and children of all ages.

The first contact often takes place in the midst of such a dense crowd that for a time one has no thought of being amazed. People walk around, discussing what they see and comparing it with their plans, and one has a tendency to imitate them. Children jump up on the fallen stones or play hide-and-seek among the uprights, and it is hard to take a few steps without coming in front of a camera aimed at someone putting his foot on a stone.

Luckily, the sky sometimes helps those who are fervently interested in the past. The weather on Salisbury Plain is remarkably changeable: It is not rare to see three or four periods of rain alternating with sunshine in a single day. With the first raindrops, the crowd quickly vanishes, leaving only a few heroic visitors huddled against uprights, more or less invisible. In the rain

*By re-erecting some of the uprights, the 1958 restoration work diminished this chaotic appearance to some extent.

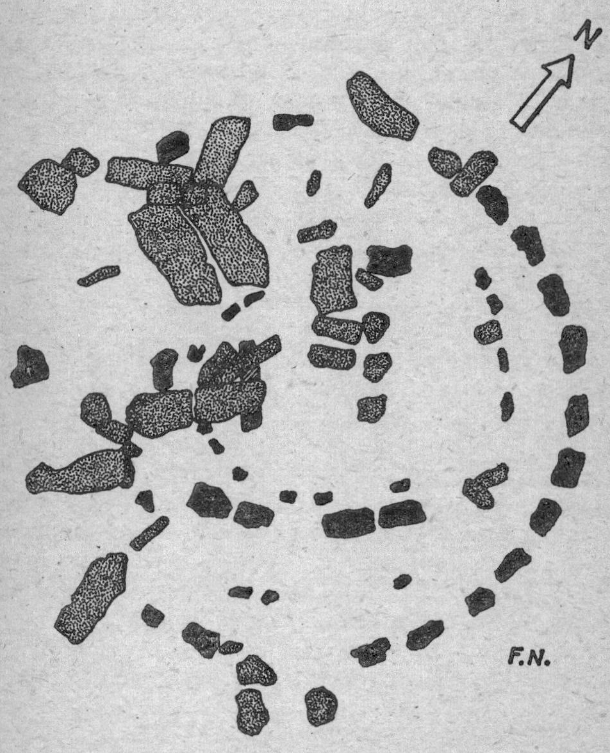

FIGURE 3—Plan of the ruins of Stonehenge as they were seen by visitors before the work of restoration.
(Solid black: standing stones. Dotted: fallen stones.)

and without a crowd, Stonehenge takes on an almost tragic appearance that takes us back more than thirty centuries. Then, after having savored the melancholy of that singular monument, the mind can begin posing its first questions.

In my experience, the dominant feeling that a visitor has, not only in the course of a single visit but also as he studies Stonehenge more thoroughly, is that he is seeing vestiges of an unknown style, period, and civilization. He cannot attach a name to the builders of that monument and is inclined to be indulgent toward those who attribute it to the gyratory motion of water in periods of glaciation, to the work of remarkably intelligent elephants, or to the Apalachee Indians!

He immediately thinks of peoples who erected dolmens and menhirs, but in spite of a few stones similar to dolmens and menhirs, that comparison is quickly abandoned. I will even say that a comparison between Stonehenge and the giant cromlech of Avebury, only 18 miles away and composed of stones with a similar origin, accentuates the contrast rather than diminishes it. And if we were to assume that one was derived from the other, we would look in vain for intermediate forms. The only common feature would be the circular shape, although the layout is perfect in one case and very irregular in the other. And when we look behind the monument, toward that vast horizon stripped by thought of all traces of contemporary civilization, we feel how alien Stonehenge is to its setting, how unsuited it is to a landscape in which the sparkling of the divine sea is lacking.

No, Stonehenge is alone, hopelessly alone, without ancestors or descendants. As Henry James said, "It stands as solitary in history as on the great plain." Comparisons have been made between its trilithons and certain monuments of the same type in Tripolitania and Arabia, but a look at drawings or photographs is enough to show how far-fetched such comparisons are. Stonehenge might as well be compared with the trilithons of the Tonga Islands! Furthermore, no peristyle like that of Stonehenge has been found anywhere. Its trilithon-peristyle combination has no equivalent, and the details of its construction strengthen the feeling that it represents one of the greatest question marks inherited from the remote past. Finally, the destruction it has suffered soon gives the impression that hope of ever finding the key to the enigma must probably be abandoned.

Let us try, however, to put a little order into the chaos that the strange structure presents at first sight.

General Outline

For convenience of description I will divide the whole formed by Stonehenge into three parts: the monument itself, its immediate vicinity, and its environs.

The monument originally included two concentric circles of upright stones: an outer one known as the Sarsen Circle and an inner one known as the Bluestone Circle. I will explain these terms later. The Sarsen Circle, often called the Outer Circle, was formed by thirty uprights with rectangular cross sections, joined in pairs by lintels. Its diameter, measured from the inner surfaces of the uprights, is nearly 100 feet. The Bluestone Circle, or Inner Circle, has a diameter of about 75 feet. It is composed of smaller and more irregularly shaped stones, undoubtedly in their natural state. It once surrounded two more concentric figures: five gigantic sarsen trilithons arranged in the shape of a horseshoe and a certain number of bluestone forming an identical shape, at the center of which was a long flat stone, lying on the ground or slightly sunk into it, known as the Altar Stone.

The monument itself was thus composed of upright stones (with one exception) that formed two shapes, the circle and the horseshoe: a bluestone circle inside a sarsen circle and a bluestone horseshoe inside a sarsen horseshoe. The sarsen uprights were joined by lintels, with separate trilithons for the horseshoe and a continuous peristyle for the circle. Despite its dilapidated condition, the whole structure gives an impression of harmony and proper proportions. It seems perfectly adapted to man's measure, sufficient to give him an idea of grandeur but without exaggeration. We will see later how all this seems to have been deliberately sought by its builders.

Let us now go beyond the enchanted circle. One of the first things we notice is the big stone by the side of the road, which usually attracts little attention from visitors arriving at Stonehenge. It deserves consideration, however, because it is perhaps the most famous stone of the whole monument: the Heel Stone. It has given rise to passionate arguments, which still continue. Its height above the ground is about 16 feet, and it leans toward the temple. Between it and the Sarsen Circle is another stone, the Slaughter Stone. It now lies flat, but in all likelihood it originally stood upright.

Another feature that is scarcely noticed by arriving visitors: a circular ditch with an inner bank that surrounds the temple at a distance of about 100 feet. This ditch is interrupted at several points, but the main gap, which probably marked the entrance of the enclosure, is on the side of the Slaughter Stone. These details can be seen in Figure 4. Inside the circular bank, small white disks now indicate the locations of some of the fifty-six holes, known as Aubrey Holes, which form a complete circle. Only those that have been excavated are marked.

Approximately on the circle formed by these holes are two low stones, situated at the ends of a diameter passing through the center of the monument. Not far from each of them, on the same circle, is a small mound. These two mounds are barely visible, especially the one on the north. They are nearly circular in shape and equidistant from the center. With the two stones, they constitute what is known as the Four Stations.

Under the grass, and therefore completely invisible, are two series of holes, each forming two circles. One of them, that of the Y and Z Holes, is outside the Sarsen Circle. The other, known as the Q and R Holes, is inside it, approximately on the circumference of the bluestones. The circles it forms are incomplete. Finally,

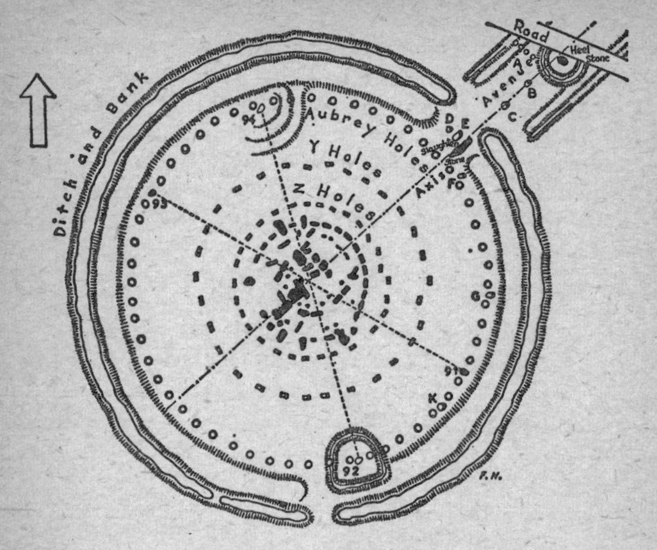

FIGURE 4—Overall plan.

British archaeologists have discovered many other holes—isolated or in groups, occupying symmetrical or asymmetrical positions in relation to the figures mentioned above—which served to hold up stones or wooden posts or were even used as graves.

The monument and its immediate vicinity are connected to what can be called the "horizon" of Stonehenge by an ancient straight road known as the Avenue, an indistinct earthwork bordered on each side by a ditch and bank. Its direction in relation to the center of the structure is the same as that of the Heel Stone, a little to the left of northeast. The horseshoes open in that direction. The Avenue continues in a straight line for about 600 yards, then divides into two branches. One branch apparently went northward to another earthwork, the Cursus, a vast, elongated enclosure with a length of 1.7 miles and an average width of 300 feet, oriented perpendicularly to that branch of the Avenue in an approximately east-west direction. As for the other branch, it seems to join the Avon or an ancient camp,

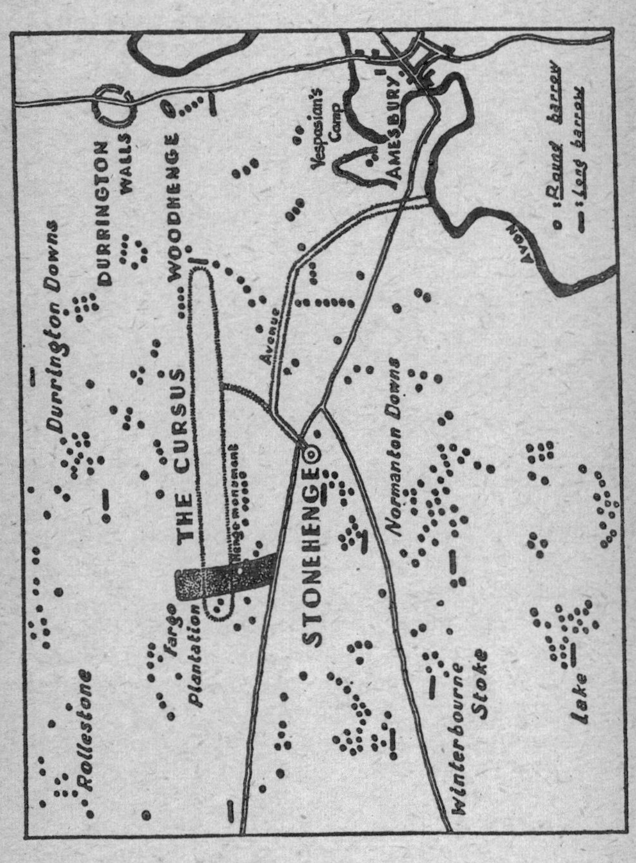

FIGURE 5—The environs of Stonehenge.

"Vespasian's Camp," just outside Amesbury, to the right on the way to Stonehenge.

Let us also note the great number of prehistoric grave mounds that are strewn over Salisbury Plain. Some, of elongated shape, are known as long barrows; the others, of circular shape, are known as round barrows and number in the hundreds. One of them, a hundred yards from Stonehenge, can be clearly seen to the left of the road a little before the Heel Stone.

About a mile and a half north of Amesbury, beside the road to Marlborough, is a curious monument named Woodhenge, which we will have occasion to discuss later. Composed of several series of holes forming concentric ellipses, it is near Durrington Walls, another vast Neolithic enclosure, but with a circular shape, which is only vaguely visible. Finally, let us note the many prehistoric vestiges—trenches, enclosures, ancient ridge roads—whose extraordinary accumulation in that region, along with that of the barrows, shows that Salisbury Plain was once heavily populated, undoubtedly much more so than it is today.

Such is the general outline of Stonehenge and its environs. It seems relatively simple, but a certain complexity will emerge as we continue our study, and more thorough examination of its various parts will reveal surprising details.

Since the middle of the nineteenth century it has been customary to designate each stone of the monument by a number. This convenient procedure avoids tedious repetitions, and one can quickly become used to it. It is used by all British authors. As can be seen in Figure 6, the series of numbers begins immediately to the right* of the monument's axis of symmetry. This axis will be defined later.

Sarsen Circle: 1 to 30, the missing stones having been given numbers.

*I will often use the expressions "to the right" or "to the left" of a certain stone or the axis of the structure. The assumption will always be that we are on the axis and looking northeast, toward the Heel Stone.

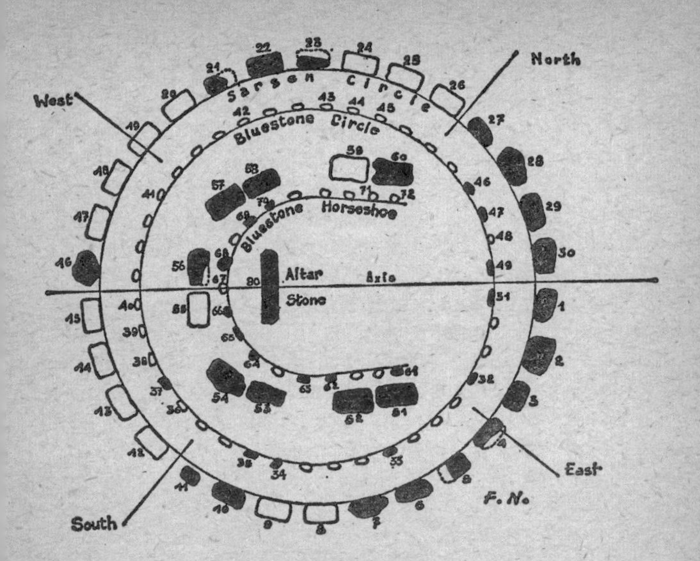

FIGURE 6—Reference plan.
(Black: stones in place. White: missing or fallen stones.)

Bluestone Circle: 31 to 49, the missing stones not being numbered.

Five sarsen trilithons: 51–52, 53–54, 55–56, 57–58, and 59–60.

Bluestone Horseshoe: 61 to 72, the missing stones not being numbered.

Four Stations: 91 to 94.

The Altar Stone (80), Slaughter Stone (95), and Heel Stone (96) have been given numbers, but they are usually designated by their names. I will follow that practice.

Each lintel has the number of one of the two uprights on which it rests, or rested, increased by 100. For example, the lintel of trilithon 59–60 is 160. This system is not often used, and neither are those I will describe below; I mention them only for the reader's information.

In the course of various excavations at Stonehenge, investigators have discovered fragments of bluestones, or holes that were used to hold up bluestones, in the lines formed by the Bluestone Circle and the Bluestone Horseshoe. These vestiges are designated by the number of the preceding stone still above the ground, followed by a letter. Thus, the holes and fragments discovered in the circle after stone 32 are designated as 32a, 32b, 32c, etc.

Finally, the series of holes are numbered in the same way: 1 to 56 for the Aubrey Holes, 1 to 30 for the Y and Z Holes.

The Sarsen Circle

Several theories have been advanced to explain the origin of the word "sarsen." It has been said to be derived from the Saxon *ses, sesen,* meaning "stone," or from the Latin *saxum,* "boulder." Reference has also been made to a local pronunciation of "sasen" for "sarsen," but the most plausible origin seems to be "Sarracen" (Saracen), a name that was once used in southern England with the rather vague meaning of "foreigner." In Cornwall and Devonshire, piles of refuse from ancient tin mines are called "Jews' leavings" or "remains of the Sarsens." Pagans in general were also called Saracens or Saresyns, and since the main specimens of sarsen stones were assembled in structures popularly attributed to pagans, such as Stonehenge and Avebury, the whole geological formation came to be known as Saracen stones, meaning "pagan stones."

Be that as it may, the word "sarsen" designates a formation belonging to the Eocene epoch, blocks of grayish sandstone scattered over the surface, mainly in the Marlborough Downs in northern Wiltshire. They are also known as greywethers. They are so numerous in some places that one can cover long distances by jumping from one to another without setting foot on the ground.

The Sarsen Circle, or Outer Circle, was originally formed by thirty upright stones. The average height of those remaining is now 13 feet 6 inches, not counting their lintels. In 1887 Flinders Petrie took exact measurements of the uprights still in place, and it is interesting to examine those measurements. The heights varied from 12 feet 8 inches for upright 21 to 14 feet 6 inches for upright 5, a difference of 1 foot 10 inches. Since the tops of the uprights are at the same level, that difference was caused by an unevenness in the ground that no longer exists. Referring to Figure 6, we see that stones 5 and 21 are almost diametrically opposite each other. Since 21 is on the side of the monument exposed to the prevailing winds on Salisbury Plain, we may conclude that they were capable of piling up large accumulations of earth at the feet of the uprights. The dimensions given by Petrie show that stones near 5 were higher than average, while those near 21 were lower than average. The figure of 13 feet 6 inches given above is the average of the heights measured by Petrie. Only one upright, 7, has exactly that height.

The inner surfaces of the stones, usually the most even, are tangent to a circle with a diameter of about 97 feet. All thirty stones were precisely placed on that theoretical circle, with an error of no more than 3 or 4 inches. They have a rectangular cross section, 7 feet by 3 feet 9 inches. They are separated by an average distance of 3 feet 6 inches, corresponding to half their width.

As I have already pointed out, the uprights of the Sarsen Circle are joined at their tops by lintels. These lintels have a length of about 10 feet 6 inches, that is, the width of an upright plus the distance between two of them. They are 3 feet 6 inches wide and 2 feet 8 inches thick. Their upper surfaces are thus 16 feet 2 inches above the ground, on the average.

Before going on I will point out that the dimensions given are approximate and may vary as much as 4 or 5 inches in some cases. The edges of the stones are not sharp and regular enough to permit greater precision. Furthermore, their cross sections vary, not being the same at ground level as several feet above it. When British authors give such figures as 7 feet by 3 feet 9 inches for the cross section of the uprights, these figures are averages. The same remarks apply to figures that will be given later.

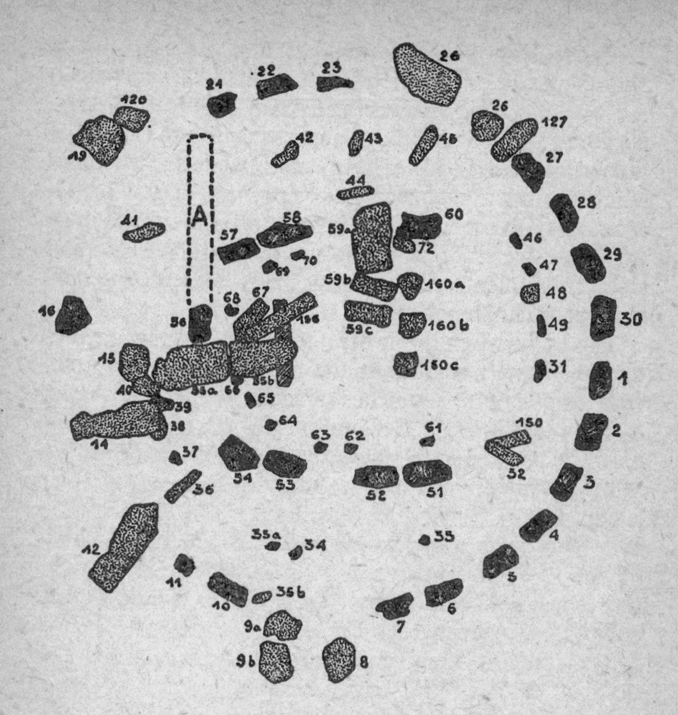

FIGURE 7—Plan of the present state of the ruins.

Of the thirty stones composing the original circle, sixteen are still in place: 1, 2, 3, 4, 5, 6, 7, 10, 11, 16, 21, 23, 27, 28, 29, and 30. (See Figure 6.) Another, 22, was restored to its upright position in 1958. Stones 27 to 30 and 1 to 7 form an uninterrupted series of eleven uprights. This is the part of the monument one sees on arriving at Stonehenge, the part that gives the illusion of a rather well preserved structure. Five lintels, three of them in succession, are still in place. A sixth, 122, connecting uprights 21 and 22, was put back in place in 1958. Uprights 12, 14, and 25 lie on the ground, 8, 9, 10, and 26 are represented only by fragments, and 13, 17, 18, 20, and 24 are missing altogether.

Many lintels are also missing. The circle originally had about thirty, of which six are still in place and two are on the ground. About twenty are therefore missing, and that is why it has been suggested that the circle of lintels may never have been completed, those stones being the last to be put in place. But that is only a supposition. The lintels of the Sarsen Circle were the most regularly shaped of all the stones in the monument and were consequently those most likely to tempt people who regarded Stonehenge as a free quarry.

The sarsen uprights were tooled in varying degrees and are usually smaller at the top than at the bottom, with a slope of 2 or 3 inches on each side. For example, a stone measuring 7 feet by 3 feet 9 inches at its base may measure 6 feet 7 inches by 3 feet 4 inches at its top. Sometimes the sides were curved to make them slightly convex, a feature known as entasis. Uprights 10 and 16 are the best examples of this refinement. The intention of obtaining a certain artistic effect is obvious. It is curious to note a prototype of the classic Greek column at Stonehenge.

The uprights were sunk into the ground an average distance of 4 feet 7 inches to 5 feet 11 inches. Their total height thus averaged about 18 feet, and their weight was about 30 tons. The depth to which they were sunk gave them normal stability, but it seems that some smaller stones were sunk much less deeply. Their stability partly depended on being connected to the stones beside them by lintels, which was probably enough to keep them standing for many centuries.

On the top of each upright were two carved protuberances, or tenons, about 3 feet 6 inches apart, center to center, a distance corresponding to the space between two uprights. These tenons fitted into mortises carved into the lower side of each lintel. They prevented any lateral movement of the lintels and fixed them firmly on top of the uprights. And the lintels were connected to each other by V-shaped joints, as shown in Figure 8.

It has been pointed out that this technique belongs to timberwork rather than stonework, especially with

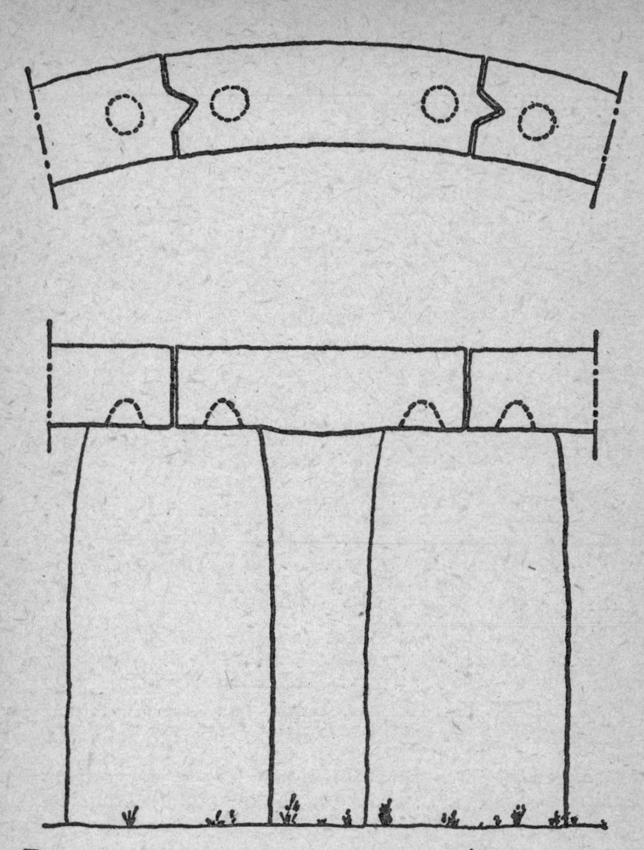

FIGURE 8—Method of assembling the lintels of the Sarsen Circle.

stones that size. It was thought that a wooden prototype must have existed at the same site or elsewhere, but none has yet been found in Western Europe except for what may have been a vague assemblage, discovered at Arminghall, near Norfolk, in Essex. There is also the hypothesis that four post holes in a straight line near the Heel Stone (at A in Figure 4), on the Avenue, may have served to hold the uprights of a triple door surmounted by wooden lintels. This would be the prototype in question, but the whole idea remains conjectural. Even if such a prototype were found, however, it would not change the fact that the way in which the lintels of the Sarsen Circle are joined is unique and peculiar to Stonehenge.

The lintels were curved in such a way as to form a perfect circle when they were assembled. The maximum difference in height among the uprights is about 4 inches, but it is believed to have been offset by variations in the thickness of the lintels. The upper surface of the lintels must thus have been almost perfectly horizontal, forming a very regular crown. It can be said that the circle of lintels was the shape in Stonehenge that came closest to perfection, the uprights being less regular, at least as far as the stonework was concerned. That perfection could scarcely have been appreciated from the ground, but perhaps it was necessary that the sun god, looking down, should be able to see a flawless example of the circle that represented him.

Let us also note the exactness of the division of the circle into thirty equal parts. If, starting from the center of the space between uprights 1 and 30, we make 12-degree divisions all around the circle, we find that each upright, augmented by the space that separates it from its neighbors, fits exactly into one of those divisions. To the people living in Wiltshire in 1300 or 1400 B.C., the Sarsen Circle and its crown of lintels must have been enough to give the illusion that Stonehenge was the work of a magician. How many peasants in our own time, on Salisbury Plain or anywhere else, could divide a circle into thirty equal parts? It is difficult if not impossible to believe that such techniques were known to the farming and pastoral tribes of more than three thousand years ago.

Certain anomalies should be mentioned. For example, one lintel has three mortises, and another has a V-shaped tenon at each end, rather than a tenon at one end and a mortise at the other. But this is unimportant and can easily be explained. It is not the same with other irregularities.

The first one is the distance between uprights 1 and 30: 4 feet, which is 6 inches greater than average.

British authors are almost unanimous in saying that this interval marked the entrance of the monument. It corresponds to the direction of the Avenue and the middle of the opening of the horseshoe. And, seen from the center of the structure, the Heel Stone is between the two uprights. It would seem, however, that if the builders wanted to mark the entrance of such an impressive monument, they might have done it in a more visible way. Six inches is not a great enough distance to be noticed immediately, especially in view of the curvature of the colonnade. We will no doubt have occasion to return to that abnormal interval later.

Another curious detail will hold our attention longer. Upright 11 measures only 8 feet above the ground, almost exactly half the height of the other uprights increased by the thickness of their lintels. The dimensions of its cross section, 4 feet by 2 feet 2 inches, are also not far from being half of those of the other uprights. Upright 11 is therefore highly unusual. In a structure as perfect as the Sarsen Circle, where all sorts of difficulties were overcome, this seems quite strange; of course, many explanations have been proposed.

One of them is that upright 11 was formed of different stones, one hard, the other soft, and that weathering caused the soft part to disintegrate, while the hard part remained. I will leave the proof or disproof of that odd hypothesis to geologists.

Another supposition is that the circle was finished at the location of upright 11, that slight errors had been made in calculating the positions assigned to the uprights in order to form a circle, and that the builders were finally confronted with a space too small for a stone of proper size. This might be given serious consideration if the alleged errors were specified, but no such errors have been found, so the supposition is gratuitous. Furthermore, estimation of the distance between uprights 10 and 12, on either side of 11—taking into account that 12 is lying on the ground—shows that a stone of normal size could have been put in that space.

It has also been said that the top part of upright 11

was broken off, possibly by lightning or by people in search of building stones. But its cross section would also have had to be reduced, and that seems inconceivable. Upright 11 has no unusual feature other than its smaller size. Aside from that, it is like all the other uprights.

Finally, the most common explanation since Flinders Petrie is that the builders ran out of material: They did not put a stone like the others in that place because they could not find one big enough. I have always been skeptical about that argument even though it has the advantage of overcoming the difficulty in a simple way. If that had been the only reason, the builders would have used a stone as close to normal size as possible; the fact is that there are stones in the Marlborough Downs larger than upright 11. And if the builders had wanted to erect an upright like the others there, they would have taken one from wherever it could be found. We will see later that it mattered little to them how far they had to go for their materials. If necessary, they would have taken a stone of a different geological nature.

Considering its height, upright 11 may quite possibly have marked a gap in the circle of lintels. Or above it there may have been a lintel twice the size of the others, 21 feet long and weighing 13 or 14 tons. That would not have been impossible since the tops of the neighboring uprights, 10 and 12, have two tenons. Or perhaps a normal upright was intended for that place and was then replaced with the present stone for unknown reasons. Excavations in that vicinity might bring a solution to the problem.

I will not describe the other singularities of upright 11. Their causes escape us, but the builders surely had serious reasons for doing what they did. Did that stone mark the entrance of the temple, as was suggested by the British author Edgar Barclay at the end of the nineteenth century? It is possible, especially since, as we will see later, there is a gap in the circular bank on the same radius as upright 11. I will mention only one detail, which may be related to its small size: The meridian of the center of the monument passes very close to its west side, at a distance of about 2 feet.

But the most surprising thing about this whole matter is the persistence with which most British investigators ignore the consequences of upright 11's small size. With the notable exception of Edgar Barclay, nearly all of them reconstruct the monument as if this upright were not different in any way. They show the circle of lintels as continuous, and upright 11 is drawn like all the others. They seem determined to overlook a fact that is obvious to anyone who sees Stonehenge.

To finish my description of the Sarsen Circle, I will point out one feature that may have been part of the "magician's" secrets: The height of the uprights augmented by the thickness of their lintels, 16 feet 2 inches, is exactly equal to one-sixth of the diameter of the circle, or one-third of its radius. If we divide that height by one-thirtieth of the circumference of the circle, that is, the width of an upright plus the interval, or 10 feet 6 inches, we obtain a ratio very close to 1.6, corresponding to the "golden mean." This ratio may explain the impression of harmony and perfect proportion given by that part of Stonehenge.

The Bluestone Circle

The Bluestone Circle is both the simplest and the most complex part of the monument. The simplest because it is probably the remains of a circle of untooled stones that could be described in a few lines. The most complex because it seems to be the most recent of several different circles, or attempts at making a circle, which go back in time at various intervals.

First of all, why the name "bluestones?" These monoliths belong to a geological formation very different from that of the sarsen stones. They are eruptive rocks, related to basalt or of the same composition as granite, known in geology as dolerite and rhyolite. They are said to have bluish glints, especially when they have been washed by rain. Of the twenty stones remaining in the circle, 16 are dolerite and 4 are rhyolite.

The Bluestone Circle is the only part of Stonehenge reminiscent of megalithic monuments of the circular cromlech type. Like them, it seems to be composed of untooled monoliths with the natural shapes of pillars or slabs, of different heights. These stones are arranged in a circle about 10 feet inside the Sarsen Circle. They were probably included in the final monument to honor an ancient tradition. As we will see later, they must have had a special virtue in the eyes of the builders.

British authors are far from being in agreement on the number of bluestones in the original circle. The following figures have been proposed: 30 (corresponding to the number of sarsen stones in the Outer Circle), 36, 39, 40 . . . This last figure, proposed for the first time by Stukeley in 1723, was almost unanimously accepted until the work carried out by the archaeologists Piggott and Atkinson in 1956, when fragments of bluestones, and holes that had held stones, were discovered. The number must now be considered as somewhere in the neighborhood of sixty. Other investigators, including Petrie, have believed that the Bluestone Circle was never finished. But let us see what remains of that part of the monument.

As shown in Figure 7, only six stones are still standing: 31, 33, 34, 46, 47, and 49; five are inclined: 32, 37, 38, 39, and 48; and seven are lying on the ground: 36, 40, 41, 42, 43, 44, and 45. If we accept the figure given by Piggott and Atkinson about forty are missing. The height of the stones varies between 2 feet 4 inches and 6 feet 7 inches, and their inside surfaces are tangent to a circle with a diameter of about 77 feet. Only stones 49 and 31, on either side of the Axis, have their outer surfaces tangent to that circle. The distance between them at their bases is 5 feet, and as in the case of uprights 1 and 30 in the Sarsen Circle, which face them, this interval is different from the others. It is smaller than average if the number of stones was forty, larger if it was close to sixty.

A curious detail: The ratio between the areas of the Sarsen and Bluestone Circles (that is, the ratio between the squares of their radii) is 1.6 to 1. Although this same ratio is found elsewhere in the structure, it may be merely a coincidence here. Application of it is more easily explained in the vertical plane than in the horizontal. But we should not be surprised by anything at Stonehenge if the whole monument was meant to be seen from above. Aside from everything else, the ratio is important because, if it was deliberately sought by the builders, it shows that they knew how to calculate the area of a circle.

Another important observation was made by Robert Newall: Most of the bluestones in the circle, whether they are upright or lying on the ground, are directly opposite another stone in relation to the center; in other words, they are arranged in pairs at opposite ends of a single diameter. Among the eighteen to twenty remaining stones, there are eight such pairs. This is strange, and Newall believed, not without reason, perhaps, that the original number of stones in the circle was not much

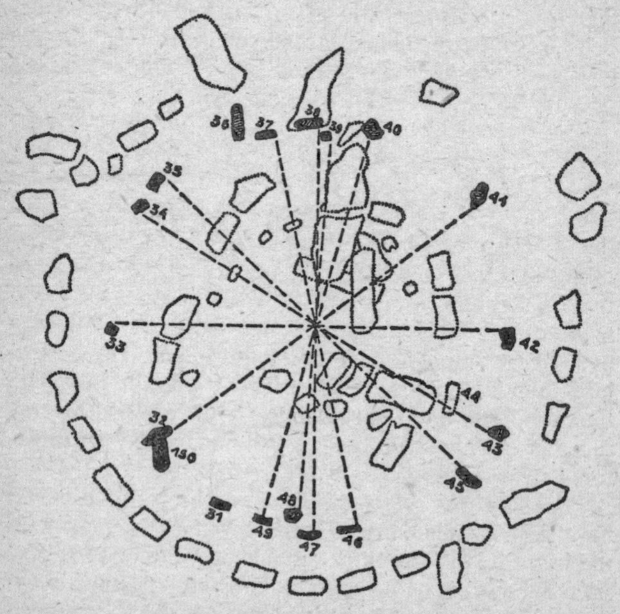

FIGURE 9—Diametrical alignments in the Bluestone Circle.

greater than the present number. If some of the stones were taken away, it is unlikely that the people who took them would have chosen them in opposing pairs.

Another observation: the four rhyolite stones, numbered 38, 40, 46, and 48 in Figure 9, are arranged in opposing pairs, 38–46 and 40–48. Although these pairs are not precisely at the ends of a single diameter, their opposition is noteworthy.

One more fact tending to support Newall's hypothesis is that each of the remaining stones is on a line of sight from the center of the monument. It would thus seem that the circle was laid out after the great trilithons were erected and that the builders then placed stones only at places from where they could see the center. Stones 36, 40, and 45 appear to be exceptions to this rule, but they are all lying on the ground, and none of them is in its original position. Furthermore, 36 has a special nature, which we will discuss later, and judging from their present location, 40 and 45 may have been on a line of sight from the center, through the intervals of trilithons 55–56 and 59–60. Only stone 33 does not seem to have been visible from the center.

The bluestones of Stonehenge have not finished posing problems for us.

Stone 32 is half lying on another bluestone, numbered 150, which has a rather puzzling feature: In one of its sides there are two holes, apparently mortises like those in the sarsen lintels; that is why it has been given a three-digit lintel number. It is 7 feet 9 inches long and slightly curved in the horizontal plane. It seems to justify the assumption that there was once at least one bluestone trilithon. For a time, however, controversy raged over that hypothetical trilithon, some investigators accepting its existence, others rejecting it.

For those who rejected it, a bluestone trilithon would have been an incongruous object, out of keeping with the beautiful symmetry of Stonehenge. Stone 150, they said, once stood as an upright, and the holes in it were intended to receive offerings. Although some envisaged a second bluestone trilithon for the sake of symmetry, the majority opinion was that there had never been even one. But who can claim to have the last word in archaeology?

Things took another turn in 1929, with a discovery made when bluestone 36 was lifted: It, too, had mortise holes, in the side that had been in contact with the ground. Then, when traces of tenons had been found at the tops of stones 67 and 70 in the horseshoe, there could no longer be any doubt that bluestone trilithons had once existed at Stonehenge. They had later been dismantled, and their lintels had been placed on end, the sides bearing the holes facing outward. We will probably never know why this was done, but in any case, the builders of the great sarsen structure seem to have been undecided as to what they should do with their bluestones.

After they had positioned the stones as they are now, here is what they may have done, or tried to do. Approximately on the line of the present circle, they may have begun making a cromlech composed of two concentric circles, the stones arranged in pairs along a single radius. (See Figure 10.) One interesting detail is that two or three extra stones seem to have been added to the pairs on either side of the Axis, as though to mark its direction and position. But after holes for that double cromlech had been dug on about half the length of the projected circles, and after stones had been placed in some of them, the project was apparently abandoned. We do not know why, but it is possible that the abandonment was caused by the erection of the sarsen structure. The holes of those two concentric figures have been named the Q and R Holes, and they constitute a phase in the construction of Stonehenge known as Stonehenge II.

There seems to have been a later attempt to make another double cromlech, but this time outside the Sarsen Circle. The bluestones were to be placed in two concentric circles of holes, the Y and Z Holes. (See Figure 4.) This project was also abandoned, and again we do not know why. The builders apparently lost hope

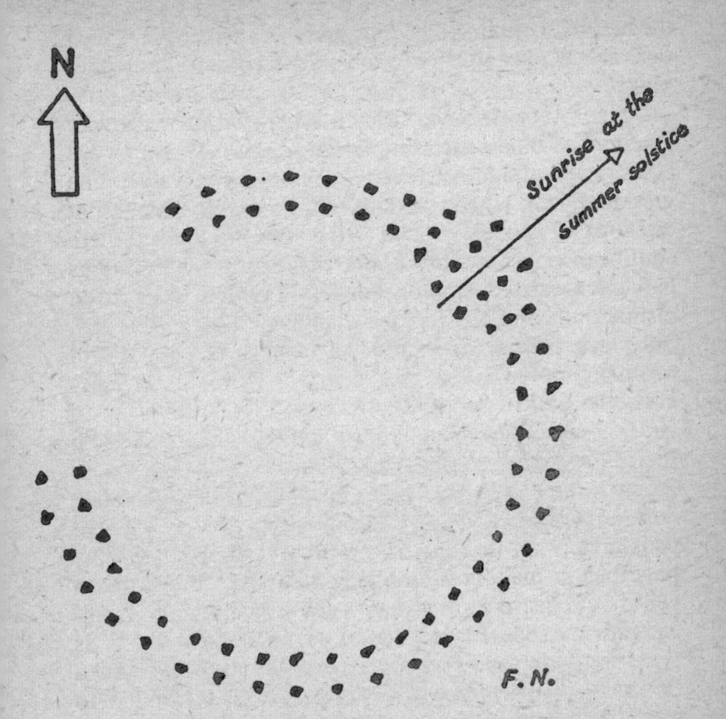

FIGURE 10—The incomplete double circle of bluestones, or Stonehenge II.
(The stones also mark the locations of the Q and R Holes.)

of succeeding in making a double cromlech and contented themselves with the figure we know today.

Excavations on the present line of bluestones have given curious results. In 1883 William Cunnington reported finding a fragment of a missing stone between 32 and 33. But later work, first by Hawley and then by Piggott, showed that there had been six bluestones between 33 and 34, eight between 40 and 41, and five between 32 and 33. It was these findings that prompted British scientists to estimate the original number of bluestones in the circle at about sixty.

There are many problems that remain to be solved,

however. Stubs of bluestones are still in the ground. Why were they broken off? Both dolerite and rhyolite are very hard. We will see later that the handling and transport of these stones placed severe demands on their hardness. If the purpose of breaking them off at the bottom was to move or destroy them, it would have been easier to widen the holes in which they stood and push them over. Attributing the breaks to awkwardness on the part of the people who transported them is not a satisfactory answer with stone of that kind.

And what are we to think of the countless bluestone chips scattered around Stonehenge, even in the Neolithic long barrows? They might suggest that there was another time like the nineteenth century, when innkeepers in the vicinity lent hammers to guests who intended to visit Stonehenge so that they could break off a piece of stone to take with them as a souvenir. The chips were not evidence of a fit of destructive madness since they are found in barrows, which were particularly respected places in prehistoric times. A block of bluestone weighing a ton was discovered in a long barrow, the Bowls Barrow, 14 miles from Stonehenge.

Many other unanswered questions come to mind. Were there really bluestone trilithons, and if so, where were they placed? Why are there now only pairs of opposing stones in the circle? Why do stones 39 and 41, unlike the others, have their outer surfaces tangent to the circle? And if we went into further detail, how many more problems would appear! The mystery of the Stonehenge bluestones remains unsolved.

The Sarsen Trilithons

Inside the Bluestone Circle stood five gigantic sarsen trilithons arranged in the shape of a horseshoe. The word "trilithon" was first used by William Stukeley. It is formed from the Greek words for "three" and "stone."

Of the five original trilithons, only two are still intact: 51–52 and 53–54. A third, 57–58, was put back in place during the restoration work of 1957–1958. Only one upright of each of the others, 55–56 and 59–60, is still standing: 56 and 60. Old drawings show upright 56, belonging to the central trilithon, leaning heavily toward the inside of the monument. It was straightened in 1901 under the direction of Professor Gowland. Upright 55 lies beside it, broken in two. The lintel that joined them is intact and can still be seen lying on the Altar Stone, with its enormous mortises.

This lintel has two depressions in its upper surface, corresponding to the mortises in its lower surface. They are probably the beginnings of mortises that were abandoned when the builders decided to make mortises on the other side, for reasons unknown to us. Some have thought, however, that they served to support the uprights of a small trilithon perched on top of the large one—an example of the many strange ideas that have been formulated with regard to Stonehenge.

Upright 60 once had a deep natural cavity at the bottom of its outer face, large enough to contain a crouching person. The cavity has been filled in with concrete. The result is an eyesore, but the operation was necessary because the upright threatened to crack all the way through and collapse. Upright 59 lies on the ground beside it, broken in three pieces. The same is true of the lintel; one piece of it was thrown more than 25 feet away from the base of the trilithon.

The five trilithons had the same width, about 15 feet 5 inches, equal to the length of the lintels that surmounted them, but their heights were different. The central trilithon, or Great Trilithon, was 25 feet 6 inches high, including its lintel, the two beside it were 21 feet 3 inches, and the two at the ends of the horseshoe were 20 feet.

At the bottom of each trilithon the space between the uprights is so narrow that a man has to turn sideways to go through it, but it widens toward the top. This seems to have been done so that anyone looking up at the trilithon would not have the impression that its uprights came together under its lintel. The uprights of the central trilithon were apparently more uniformly spaced, however, judging from the shape of upright 56.

Some British authors believe that they were also more widely spaced than those of the other trilithons, whose separation is estimated at 12 to 16 inches. The space between them is said to have been from 2 feet 6 inches to 3 feet 6 inches, the most likely figure being midway between those two extremes, about 3 feet. We will see how debatable that conclusion is. Finally, as I have already indicated, the lintels were fixed to the uprights like those of the Sarsen Circle by means of mortises and tenons.*

The sarsen trilithons are the most impressive part of Stonehenge. A drawing or photograph of one of them nearly always appears on the cover or frontispiece of books on the monument. That unique shape is immediately recognizable. It is found nowhere but in that area of Wiltshire, and in it we sense the mark of the great master builder who presided over construction of the sanctuary.

Here the magician showed his skill as an illusionist because each element gives the impression of being higher than it actually is. How was this effect obtained? It is, of course, a matter of proportion. If we divide the height of the central trilithon by its width, the result is 1.66. For the other trilithons, the figures are 1.33 and 1.4. This seems to have been calculated in advance since the elements had the same width. And to obtain that effect, the builders did not hesitate to sacrifice stability. Thus, upright 56 of the Great Trilithon sinks into the earth to a depth of 7 feet 7 inches, while its companion, 55, was buried only to a depth of 3 feet. This imbalance may have caused the fall of that magnificent structure. As for trilithon 57–58, now restored, its uprights extended such a short distance into the ground

*This method of fixing one stone on top of another by means of mortises and tenons is not peculiar to Stonehenge. At Delphi I saw stones with identical tenons on their upper sides. The same method was also used on Minorca for the bilithons known as *taoulas,* whose top slabs are joined to their supports in that way. And it is essentially the same method used on Easter Island to secure the stone cylinders that surmount some of the famous statues.

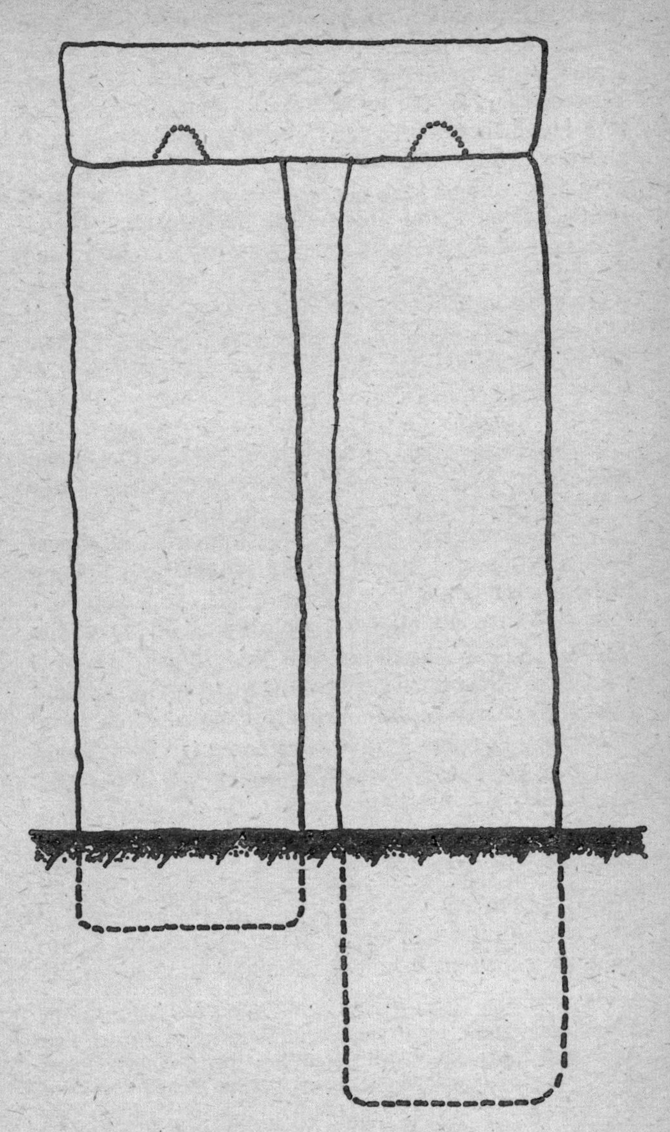

FIGURE 11—The Great Trilithon.

that it is a wonder it remained standing till 1797, when it finally fell.

It is worth noting that the architect must have foreseen the imbalance caused by the difference in depth between the uprights of the Great Trilithon. At the base of 55, the one now lying on the ground, a distinct protuberance made the buried part larger than the part above it. There was thus a kind of widened foundation to compensate for the lack of depth. This precaution proved to be inadequate, but the problem had been studied.

To return to the question of proportions in the vertical plane, there is one element that must obviously be taken into account: variations in ground level. Let us take the example of trilithon 53–54. In about 1810, Colt Hoare measured its height as 20 feet 8 inches. In 1880, with Petrie's precise measurements, its height was set at 21 feet 2 inches, and it is about the same today. The level of the ground at the foot of the trilithon therefore sank 6 inches, for there is no reason to doubt the accuracy of Colt Hoare's measurements. The same remarks apply to the other trilithons and uprights of the Sarsen Circle. As I have already said, exposure to the prevailing winds is probably the cause of these variations. We therefore cannot obtain rigorous accuracy in the vertical relations I have indicated, but the approximation is such that it allows us to assume that those relations were deliberately sought.

We must also take into account the limited distance from which a trilithon could be seen in its entirety. The central trilithon, for example, could not be wholly seen from more than 72 feet. Beyond that distance, it was partially or completely hidden by various other parts of the monument. The same is true, in different degrees, of the other trilithons. All their dimensions and proportions must have been determined in relation to the maximum distance of total visibility. In the case of the Great Trilithon, its distance from the center of the monument was exactly equal to its height, which was about one-third of the maximum distance from which it could be seen entirely, which probably applies to the other trilithons, also. We do not know with certainty that the architect calculated such effects, but if so, he was remarkably successful.

And that does not seem to be the only architectural or esthetic refinement in the design of the trilithons. As in the case of the uprights in the Sarsen Circle, their sides are curved outward. Upright 56 of the central trilithon is the best example of this. It is one of the most impressive and elegant monoliths I have ever seen, and it makes me regret all the more that its companion upright and the lintel that joined them have fallen. The complete trilithon must have been a striking sight. With its 22-foot height above the ground and its total height of 29 feet 6 inches, stone 56 is the second largest monolith in Great Britain, the highest being the Rudstone, at Rudstone on the Wolds, in Yorkshire.

In France, higher menhirs are rather numerous. Besides the great menhir at Locmariaquer, which measured 77 feet, weighed 300 tons, and now lies on the ground, broken in four pieces, there are a score of standing stones whose height above ground is greater than that of stone 56 at Stonehenge. But the conditions in which that superb monolith was erected will increase our astonishment and admiration still more.

Another example of the Stonehenge architect's skill is given by the lintel of trilithon 53–54. It is carved in the shape of an inverted truncated pyramid to attenuate the effects of perspective. The dimensions of its upper sides are greater than those of its lower side. The lintels of the other trilithons were less well fashioned, even that of the central trilithon. The lintel of 51–52 is streaked with grooves and spotted with holes in which birds make their nests. I saw a nest of starlings between a tenon and its mortise.

The lintels of the trilithons weighed between 10 and 12 tons. To the best of my knowledge, that is the weight record for isolated stones perched at such a height. No dolmen has an upper slab more than 13 feet above the ground. At Mycenae, however, shortly before the construction of Stonehenge, a stone weighing close to 100 tons was placed at a height of more than 20 feet: the lintel of the door of "Agamemnon's tomb."

The Bluestone Horseshoe

As with the stones that composed the circle, British authors have never been in agreement on the original number of bluestones in the horseshoe inside the line of great trilithons. There were twelve according to some, fifteen according to others, arranged symmetrically in groups of three in front of each trilithon. A few authors placed the number at seventeen, but the generally accepted figure is now nineteen, proposed by Stukeley. On each branch of the horseshoe, certain stones correspond to empty spaces on the other side. It is thus rather easy to count nineteen stones or spaces for stones.

The stones are dolerite and therefore of the same geological nature as those of the circle. But they differ in one important respect: They were given a conical shape, like a kind of obelisk. In some cases their tops are flattened, and as I have said, stones 67 and 70 show traces of tenons. Their average weight must be about 3½ tons. Stones 67 and 68 weigh a little more than 4 tons.

The rounded part of the horseshoe has a diameter of about 39 feet and originally included eleven stones, while each branch had four. The extremities of the branches more or less coincide with those of trilithons 51–52 and 59–60. The stones are about 6 feet 6 inches apart. Their height above the ground varies from 6 feet for stone 61 to 9 feet 3 inches for stone 67. The latter, at the center of the curve, is now lying on the ground. It was probably knocked over by the fall of upright 55 and the lintel of the central trilithon.

The average diameter of the stones is about 2 feet. Like those of the sarsen trilithons, their heights diminished as their distance from the Axis increased. Of the original nineteen stones, twelve are left, of which six are intact and still in place: 61, 62, 63, 68, 69, and 70. The broken stubs of 64 and 65 barely rise above the ground. Stone 66 is under the fragments of upright

55 of the central trilithon, and 67, 71, and 72 are lying on the ground. Seven stones are missing. Stone 67 was apparently the highest since it was in the middle. It and the Altar Stone are the only two on the Axis.

There would be little to say about the Bluestone Horseshoe if two of its stones did not have a rather disconcerting feature: 68 and 66, equidistant from the Axis. Stone 66 now exists only as a broken stub, but it can still be seen that it had a longitudinal protuberance with the same dimensions as a groove that extends along the full height of 68. These are the elements of the tongue-and-groove joint that is used, for example, to join floorboards.

Were the two stones originally connected? Many British authors think so, and there is a good chance that they are right. But it would then seem that the builders deliberately made difficulties for themselves because, once again, this system is better adapted to working with wood than with stone. It is understandable that the lintels of the Sarsen Circle should be assembled by a system copied from one used with wood, but the tongue-and-groove system of bluestones 66 and 68 remains inexplicable. Why should it have been used with wood? Two posts joined in that way would achieve no practical purpose. A wooden prototype therefore seems excluded, at least with regard to those two stones. Did their joining have a symbolic meaning? Probably, but what was it? It would be interesting to look for analogies, even far away from Salisbury Plain.

The Altar Stone

The Altar Stone, 15 feet 9 inches long and 3 feet 3 inches wide, lies on the ground, slightly buried, and is now broken in two pieces. Its length is close to the height of the Sarsen Circle and a sixth of its diameter. Many people have dug under it in search of treasure, but Stukeley did so for a more scientific purpose and measured its thickness at 1 foot 9 inches.

Some authors have suggested that it once stood as an upright. Atkinson has shown that one of its ends was beveled, which would have made it easier to fit into a hole. I will point out in passing, however, that beveling the buried end of an upright stone is not the best way to assure its stability. In my opinion, the question of whether or not the Altar Stone was originally upright is still undecided. In the present state of things, there is no reason to assume that it was. The problem may be solved if the central trilithon is ever restored. The Altar Stone bears a name that irritates archaeologists, but there is really no need to be upset over it.

Because of its shape and dimensions, especially its small thickness, it does not seem to belong to either the sarsen or the bluestone structure. It is composed of a kind of micaceous sandstone of which there are hardly any other examples in Stonehenge. Its present position in relation to the Axis is slightly oblique: Its long sides form an angle of 6½ degrees with a line perpendicular to the Axis. Since a fragment of upright 55 of the central trilithon is lying on it, its break and displacement were probably caused by the fall of that upright.

Wishing to determine this more precisely, I reproduced the fall of the Great Trilithon by means of a scale model. The Altar Stone in the model was displaced in the way described above. It is therefore quite likely that it originally had a symmetrical position in relation to the Axis. It would be rather surprising, in fact, if it had not.

The Altar Stone seems to have been given its present name by Inigo Jones. It has often been said that there is no justification for it. This is partially true, but that is no reason to treat the stone with disdain, going so far as to ignore the fact that it is broken in two, or showing its obliquity, in certain plans, as the opposite of what it actually is.

By its location, nature, and size, the Altar Stone is unique in Stonehenge. We must therefore assume that it had a special purpose, and if I had to choose a hypothesis, I would prefer one that would confirm its name. Let us not forget that archaeologists are nearly unanimous in believing that Stonehenge was a temple.

The Y and Z Holes

When we study the work done at Stonehenge by British scientists, we are surprised by the large number of holes revealed by excavations. They are generally small and were dug into the underlying chalk. They were later covered over by earth and grass, becoming invisible. But they still exist, and their number gives the impression that the ground inside and outside the monument was riddled with holes of varying depths.

Most of them were discovered by probing with a metal blade that sank into the ground easily or with a certain resistance, depending on whether the chalk had been hollowed out or not. Archaeologists were able to ascertain that some holes had held wooden posts and others stones, but the purpose of many could not be determined. Graves with bones in them were also found. Among these cavities the most distinctive, in terms of their number and the circular figure they form, are the Q and R Holes, the Y and Z Holes, and the Aubrey Holes.

I will describe the latter in the section on the ditch and bank. For the moment, I will point out that they have a certain relation to the name of the Y and Z Holes. When they were first discovered, they were called the X Holes since their number was then unknown. They were later called the Aubrey Holes, from the name of the man who had first reported them. Then, when two more series of holes were discovered shortly afterward, the same method of naming them was used: The letters representing the other unknowns of an equation were assigned to them.

The Y and Z Holes were meant to hold three-quarters of the bluestone structure, after the sarsen structure had been erected. There were to be two circles, with a radius of 60 feet 6 inches for the Z Holes and 90 feet 7 inches for the Y Holes. These radii, taken from the center of the monument, are rather irregular, however, some of them being as much as 4 feet too short and others as much as 8 feet too long.

In each circle the number of holes is thirty, corresponding to the number of uprights in the Sarsen Circle. They have been numbered in the same way. Hole Z–7 is in the ramp that was used for erecting the corresponding sarsen stone, number 7. Hole Z–8 was not dug, but the position it was to have occupied more or less coincides with the fragments of upright 8 in the Sarsen Circle. Some authors have therefore wondered if these holes were not dug after destruction of the monument had already begun. Their horizontal dimensions are about 6 feet by 8 feet, and their depth varied from 2 feet 11 inches for the Y Holes to 3 feet 5 inches for the Z Holes. I do not know if the fifty-nine holes have all been exactly located.

Eighteen holes in each circle have so far been excavated. These excavations have given meager results: a few sarsen chips, usually one bluestone chip in each hole, fragments of British-Roman pottery, all this mingled with lumps of chalk and earth from the digging. One hole contained five tines of deer antlers carefully placed on the bottom. These finds gave the impression that the Y and Z Holes were relatively recent. Actually, however, they seem to date from about the same time as the sarsen structure. They are thought never to have received the bluestones for which they were dug.

A few words about the graves. One of them was found near hole Y–9, the other inside the monument, between bluestones 49 and 31. The first, dating from the Roman period, contained a skeleton whose bones had been broken to make them fit into a hole too small for them. The second contained remains that had been disturbed by previous excavations. It is thought to be rather ancient. Other bodies may have been buried around Stonehenge, judging from certain drawings made in the eighteenth century, which I will discuss in the second part of this book.

I have already referred to the Q and R Holes. I will here say simply that their incomplete circle extended approximately from upright 28 to upright 16.

The Four Stations

We have seen that the Four Stations are formed by two stones and two mounds. They are situated at the ends of two straight lines of equal length that run through the center of the monument with an angle of 45 degrees between them. This precision is undoubtedly too great to have been accidental. At first sight, it seems that the Four Stations were placed on a circle whose center coincided exactly with that of the monument. The builders would thus have known how to inscribe a regular eight-sided polygon in a circle. But it may also be that they wanted to mark the corners of a rectangle whose diagonals intersected at the center of the monument.

The Four Stations call for the following remarks:

1. They are placed on a circle with a radius of 142 feet.

2. Lines connecting adjacent stations, that is, mound 92 to stone 91 and stone 93 to mound 94, are parallel to the axis of the monument.

3. None of the stations could be seen from the center of the monument. From each of them, the one opposite it was invisible since the stones of the monument blocked the line of sight.

4. They occupy symmetrical positions in relation to the Heel Stone.

5. They are at the corners of a large rectangle measuring 262 feet 3 inches by 108 feet 8 inches. The long sides of this rectangle pass very close to the outer edge of the Sarsen Circle. We may wonder why they are not actually tangent to that circle. They would have been if the diagonals had been made four or five feet shorter.

It is almost certain that the theoretical locations of the Four Stations played an important part in drawing up the plan of Stonehenge. The circle on which they are placed, or the rectangle they delimit, was laid out before the monument was built. They are undoubtedly not ornamental or purely symbolic accessories. The precision of the figures they form suggests that they were geographical or topographical markers.

The two mounds are often called barrows, but they are recognized as having been the locations of stones that have now disappeared. Before the nineteenth century, they were always described as holes, cavities, or depressions. Their present form may have been the result of movements of earth during excavations, notably those of Colt Hoare in about 1810. He discovered traces of cremation in mound 94. As for mound 92, Hawley found not only a hole 4 feet deep but also the inclined plane, toward the bottom of the hole, that had been used to erect the stone. It seems that stations 92 and 94 were originally upright stones surrounded at a certain distance by a circular bank of earth and a shallow ditch.

The ditch around station 92 can still be clearly seen, but the one around station 94 is scarcely visible. It would be hard for a visitor to recognize it if it were not shown on a plan. The little ditch around station 92 is not exactly circular; it is "flattened" where it touches the big bank. A perfect circle would have had to go down into the big ditch.

The two remaining stones are of different heights. Stone 91 is 9 feet high and lies on the ground. In the eighteenth century it was only tilted toward the ditch. In 1740 Stukeley wrote, "The two stones within the vallum are very small stones, and were ever so. The one stands; the other leans a little, probably from some idle people digging about it." Thirty years later, John Smith described it as still leaning toward the ditch.

Stone 93 is only 4 feet high. Both stones bear traces of deliberate shaping and are composed of sarsen.

Students of Stonehenge have wondered if the stones of the Four Stations were the only ones placed in the circle. Holes situated very close to it have recently been discovered. Judging from their size, they could have been used to hold upright stones. They are marked F, K, and G in Figure 4. Unfortunately, their positions do not make it possible to ascertain a geometrical division of the circle. Perhaps the question will eventually be settled by further investigation.

We will later discuss another stone, symmetrical with the Heel Stone in relation to the center of the monument, which may have been erected near the bank, according to early authors. A piece of it is said to have been found a foot below the ground. Information gathered on the subject seems to indicate that the stone was situated exactly on the circle of the Four Stations.

The Ditch and Bank and the Aubrey Holes

Almost nothing remains of the bank inside the circular ditch. Nowhere does it rise more than 2 feet above the ground. It is nearly indistinguishable. The ditch is still clearly visible, but it was less important, its only function being to provide material for making the bank. Excavations have shown that it was actually a series of irregularly joined ditches of varying lengths. Its depth was also irregular, varying from 4 feet 4 inches to 7 feet. That does not indicate poor workmanship; it simply shows that only the bank was important.

The bank was originally about 6 feet high and 13 to 20 feet thick. It was interrupted in three places, which can be situated in relation to the center of the monument as follows: slightly to the left of northeast and northwest for the first two, south for the third. The last gap is opposite stone 11 of the Sarsen Circle. It is also very near the little ditch around station 92. In the opinion of all authors, the northeast gap seems to have marked the main entrance of the enclosure.

The south gap must also have had a function. It and the northeast gap correspond to two features of the monument: The northeast one corresponds to the axis of symmetry, at least approximately; the south one corresponds to stone 11, which implies a break in the circle of lintels or an "anomaly" in the circle of sarsen uprights. It may be that one of the gaps was an entrance into the sacred enclosure, the other an exit. As for the third gap, it is not shown in Figure 4 because of its uncertain nature.

As far as we can judge from the present state of the site, the circle described by the bank is fairly regular. Different authors give different dimensions for it, but the following diameters are at least close approximations: inner edge of the bank: 300 feet; outer edge of the ditch: 372 feet; junction of the bank and the ditch: 337 feet.

If we measured from the middle of the bank, we would have a diameter of about 318 feet. The bank is about 98 feet from the Sarsen Circle. But the centers of the two circles do not coincide. The center of the monument is about 3 feet north-northeast of the center of the bank, which in itself would seem to indicate that the two structures were made at different times.

Half of the ditch was explored more than fifty years ago by Colonel Hawley. Eighty deer-antler picks and several shovels made of ox shoulderblades were found. These must have been tools that were used to dig the ditch and then abandoned when worn out. Excavation also brought to light fragments of Neolithic pottery, bluestone chips, several flints, and bones of animals that had probably been eaten. Since the bluestone chips were found at a depth at which the ditch had been half filled in, the ditch and bank would seem to be older than the monument. I do not know if the other half of the ditch has yet been excavated.

Just inside the bank is a circle of fifty-six holes, the Aubrey Holes. We will see how they were discovered. Their purpose is not clearly known, but they do not seem to have been used for holding upright stones or wooden posts. They were thus not part of an ancient cromlech that was later dismantled, although there are circles of stones surrounded by a ditch and bank in Great Britain. The Aubrey Holes were probably ritual pits dug for a religious or ceremonial purpose.

They are all placed on a circle with a diameter of 286 feet whose center coincides with that of the bank. Their distribution is fairly regular. They are dug at intervals of about 16 feet, and none of them has its center more than 1½ feet from the circle. They have an average diameter of 3 feet 6 inches and a depth of 3 feet 3 inches.

At least thirty-four of them have been excavated. These are marked on the ground with white disks. The excavations have not yielded results of any great interest. The contents of the holes are not uniform, except that nearly all of them contained charred human bones, scattered or in compact masses. There were also fragments of charred wood, bone needles, pieces of flint rods, and many sarsen and bluestone chips. The latter show that the stone structure is later than the Aubrey Holes and the ditch and bank.

The holes, ditch, and bank constitute a clearly defined, independent monument of which there are many other examples in England. They are called henge monuments, from the name of Stonehenge itself. They have a ditch and bank with a more or less geometrical shape, usually circular, bordered inside with a series of holes, and they always have one or more entrances. This is what we find at Stonehenge. It is called Stonehenge I by British archaeologists since it is regarded as the first phase. There could have been no simpler choice of material: This kind of monument was made solely by movements of earth. Stonehenge I apparently dates from three or four centuries before the sarsen structure.

The builders of the greater Stonehenge seem to have cared little about the circle formed by the bank and the holes. Only the exceptional location of the henge monument appears to have interested them. In Figure 4 it can be seen that the center of the main opening in the bank, facing northeast, does not coincide with the Axis. The difference is about 7 degrees. And the Four Stations almost overlap some of the Aubrey Holes; the little ditch surrounding station 92 passes through one of them. The builders may have regarded the ditch, bank, and holes as rather bothersome elements. It is possible, however, that the enclosure formed by the bank served to contain the crowds that came to witness ceremonies performed in the temple.

The Slaughter Stone

It is a sarsen stone lying on the ground, 21 feet 6 inches long, 6 feet 11 inches wide, and 2 feet 11 inches thick. It is near the south edge of the northeast entrance through the bank and ditch. Its near end is 136 feet from the center of the monument. It must have once stood erect on its other end, more or less at its present location.

It was once thought that the Slaughter Stone was the only survivor of a group of four stones that had been erected in a square. This view seems to be supported by a drawing that Inigo Jones made in about 1620 (Figure 18), showing two stones on each side of the gap in the bank.

Not much attention would have been paid to this drawing—which shows six trilithons of equal height arranged in a hexagon—if it had not been partially confirmed by another drawing made forty years later by John Aubrey, apparently on the basis of firsthand observation (Figure 19). It shows not four but three stones at the gap in the ditch.

Later, no trace of those other stones could be found, and Stukeley discredited the idea of their existence. It was not until 1923 that a hole was found in which another stone may have stood facing the Slaughter Stone. This hole is marked E in Figure 4. But John Aubrey was a conscientious observer. It may be that at the time when he made his drawings some stones from the monument, ready to be broken up and taken away, had been temporarily placed near the Slaughter Stone.

Be that as it may, the general opinion at present is that the Slaughter Stone originally stood upright. This is important, as we will see later. In the early nineteenth century, Colt Hoare and Cunnington noticed that the part of the stone that had once been buried was rough, while the rest of it was smoother and had been tooled like the stones of the main structure. Today this difference is no longer apparent, at least on the exposed part, because of the constant trampling of visitors.

There is almost unanimous agreement that the Slaughter Stone had a companion, but unfortunately the distance between the two stones can no longer be accurately ascertained.

Judging from its present position, the Slaughter Stone stood halfway between the Heel Stone and the Sarsen Circle. It now lies at the bottom of a small depression that is formed by a low bank and seems to have been made for it, though it probably resulted from the shifting of earth by excavators.

The name of the Slaughter Stone was apparently invented by Stukeley. It is odd that the name was not applied to the Altar Stone, whose position and shape would make it better adapted to animal or human sacrifices. But it does not have the "channels for the blood of victims" that can be pointed out on the Slaughter Stone, which also had the advantage, it has been said, of allowing sacrifices to be seen by a greater number of people. All this is based on nothing but imagination, but such unverified and unverifiable judgments are long-lived. Despite the commendable efforts of archaeologists, people will go on talking for a long time about the sacrifices, human or animal, performed on the Slaughter Stone. The best thing would be to place it erect again in its ancient hole.

The Heel Stone

This, as I have already said, is the most famous stone in the monument. It is a big sarsen block 20 feet long, with one end buried to a depth of 3 feet 11 inches, so that its height above the ground is 16 feet 1 inch, which is almost exactly the same as the height of the Sarsen Circle. Its cross section, at least at ground level, has the shape of an imperfect ellipse inscribed in a rectangle 9 feet by 6 feet 11 inches. It stands at a distance of 256 feet from the center of the monument and 338 feet from stations 92 and 93. It weighs more than 35 tons. It leans inward at an angle of about 17 degrees. It is not known whether this inclination was intentional.

Around the stone, at a distance of 11 feet, are traces of a small circular ditch whose purpose is unknown.

The fame of the Heel Stone comes from the following fact: If one looks toward it from the center of Stonehenge, it appears in the opening formed by uprights 1 and 30 of the Sarsen Circle and their common lintel. And if one stands at the center on the morning of June 21, one sees the sun rise a little to the left of the top of the Heel Stone, then appear above it a few minutes later, when it has emerged a little more than halfway. This was noticed long ago, and it has always struck the imagination. And I will probably not surprise the reader by saying that it has given rise to a great deal of debate, which still continues. But before we go any farther, a few explanations may be necessary.

The sun does not rise at the same point every day. Twice a year, on March 21 and September 23, it rises exactly in the east, as seen from any point on the globe. If we observe it from the same place on successive days after March 21, we will see it rise a little more to the left each morning. The difference is slight from day to day, but it is quite distinct at the end of a week, and the higher the latitude of the point of observation, the more rapidly the difference increases. Similarly, if we watch the sun go down, we will see it set a little more to the right each evening. At noon it will be a little higher in the sky each day, so that the shadow of a vertical stick will become progressively shorter after March 21. And of course this increase in the length of the sun's course across the sky is accompanied by an increase in the length of the day.

Finally, as we approach June 21, the positions of sunrise and sunset appear to become almost stationary, and this impression is stronger at higher latitudes. The differences are small, but at the latitude of southern England they are still discernible. June 21, the longest day of the year, is the summer solstice. The etymology of the word "solstice"—from the Latin *solstitium,* a combination of *sol* and *statio*—seems to stress that impression of immobility.

After June 21, the point of sunrise appears to move

again, but this time toward the right, until it finally reaches the same position as on March 21, which occurs on September 23, the second or autumnal equinox. On that date the sun again rises exactly in the east, and day and night are of equal duration. The sun continues its movement to the right until it reaches an extreme point symmetrical with its position on June 21 in relation to its equinoctial rises. It is now December 22, the winter solstice, the shortest day of the year. On that date, the shadow of a vertical stick at noon reaches its maximum length. The angle formed by the positions at which the sun rises on September 23 and December 22 is exactly the same as between June 21 and September 23. After December 22, the sun begins moving to the left again and continues until it reaches the point corresponding to March 21.

The angle formed on a given day by the direction of the rising sun with the north-south direction, or meridian, is not the same everywhere. That angle, called the azimuth, varies with latitude. It becomes smaller as latitude increases. And the angle formed by sunrises at their extreme points on June 21 and December 22 becomes greater as latitude increases. In France, it varies from about 65°30′ at Perpignan to about 78°30′ at Dunkirk.

This remarkable phenomenon, caused by the earth's inclination on its axis of rotation, generally passes unnoticed. It is curious to note how often it is unknown or misunderstood even among cultivated people, although it was well known to Chaldean shepherds and the builders of dolmens. Many people are aware that the sun rises "in the east," but that is as far as their knowledge of the subject goes. Modern progress has completely disrupted the conditions under which ancient societies lived. Today the sun no longer counts except when one wants to go out for a walk. It has been replaced by the watch and the calendar. Artificial light has eliminated night. And we tend to assume that ancient peoples shared our ignorance of, or indifference to, the shift of sunrise on the horizon. It is hard for us to understand why anyone should have used fixed reference points to mark the positions of the rising sun, particularly its extreme positions, at certain times of the year. But let us imagine for a moment what our lives would be like if all our instruments for measuring time suddenly ceased to function.

There is nothing extraordinary about the fact that at the summer solstice the rising sun can be seen above the Heel Stone from the center of Stonehenge. It would be extraordinary if there were nothing of that kind in such a monument. And since the horseshoes of the trilithons and the bluestones open in the direction of the Heel Stone, the whole structure is oriented toward the rising sun at the summer solstice. This orientation, deliberately sought by the builders of Stonehenge, is almost unanimously accepted. But there is disagreement on the function of the Heel Stone. With regard to that point we must consider another astronomical phenomenon.

There is another movement of the position of the rising sun; it is much less rapid, not even discernible in the course of a human lifetime, but quite noticeable after several centuries. It is a yearly movement, rather than a daily one. Its direction is to the right of an observer facing east. Every year, at the same time and place, sunrise is a little farther to the right. The difference is very small, less than a minute of angle every century. (A minute of angle corresponds to one inch seen from a distance of 300 feet.) It is caused by rather complex astronomical phenomena that would take too long to describe here. If the reader is unfamiliar with the precession of the equinoxes, as the movement is called, I will ask him simply to accept the fact that it exists.

We must at least be aware of its existence in order to understand the controversies to which the Heel Stone has given rise, as well as the problem it poses. Here is the problem: Let us assume that Stonehenge was built 3,500 years ago. If at that time it was oriented toward sunrise at the summer solstice, the direction of that sunrise should not be now what it was then. From the center of the monument there should be a shift to the right of close to 3 feet. So if the observation point was behind the Great Trilithon, as is generally assumed, and if the top of the Heel Stone marked the direction in which the sun rose above the horizon at the summer solstice, the sun ought to rise to the right of the top of the Heel Stone on the morning of June 21 in our time. But it does not: It rises about a foot and a half to the left.

It would thus seem that the Heel Stone has never marked the point of sunrise on the longest day of the year. British archaeologists tend to deny any connection between that stone and the orientation of the monument toward sunrise at the summer solstice despite the incredulity of the thousands of people who come every year on the morning of June 21 to see the sun appear behind the Heel Stone. I will return to these questions later, but for the moment I will point out that the British archaeologists' view is based on some rather debatable assumptions; for example:

1. That the direction of sunrise was considered to be determined by the point at which the upper edge of the sun first appeared above the horizon.
2. That the observation point was behind the Great Trilithon.
3. That sunrise was marked by the peak of the Heel Stone.

As for the stone itself, it shows no trace of tooling but seems to have been chosen for its shape. Seen from the center of the monument, its axis of symmetry nearly coincides with a vertical line passing through its peak. There is said to be a difference of 4 or 5 inches between the distances from that line to the outer edges, but it is not noticeable to the naked eye; furthermore, the matter needs to be re-examined. For a man of average height standing on the Altar Stone, the peak of the Heel Stone coincides with the horizon. If that is not accidental, the inclination of the stone toward the temple would seem to have been deliberate, but the opposite view is also tenable.

In the second part of this book we will see why it is called the Heel Stone or the Friar's Heel. Some British authors mention other names that have been applied to it. One of them, the Hele Stone, is rather difficult to explain. Suggested origins are "hell," the Greek word *helios,* "sun," and the Saxon word *helan,* "to hide," since the sun if first hidden behind the stone, then appears above it at the summer solstice. The latter explanation was the one accepted by Petrie. The stone is also called the Index Stone and the Sun Stone. It is worth noting that a dolmen near Portisham, in Dorset, is called the Hellstone. Another suggestion is that the name is a corruption of the Celtic *freas heol,* a contracted form of *cloch na freas heol,* "stone of the rising sun." In view of its importance and fame, I will continue to call the stone by its most common name: the Heel Stone.

The Avenue

The Avenue is a broad roadway bordered on each side by a ditch and bank. It runs in a straight line for several hundred yards, more or less in the direction of the Axis. Its width is about 40 feet between the two banks and 72 feet between the centers of the ditches. It was reported for the first time by Stukeley, who described it as follows:

> The Avenue of Stonehenge was never observ'd by any who have wrote of it, tho' a very elegant part of it, and very apparent. It answers . . . to the principal line of the whole work, the north-east, whereabouts the sun rises, when the days are longest.
>
> The Avenue extends itself, somewhat more than 1700 feet, in a straight line down to the bottom of the valley, with a delicate descent.
>
> I observe the earth of the ditches is thrown inward, and seemingly some turf on both sides, thrown upon the Avenue: to raise it a little above the level of the downs.

The two ditches continue perfectly parallel to the bottom, 40 cubits (i.e., 69 ft. 4 in.) asunder.

Lucky Stukeley, to have found the Avenue "very apparent!" Today it is nearly invisible; first it is cut by the road; then it is lost among the fields. One must know where to look for it in order to make it out, and I cannot say if its straight part is still visible in its entirety from the center of the monument.

Measurements have shown that it is perfectly straight and that its sides are exactly parallel. Since it runs straight for about 2,000 feet and may not have been visible for its entire length, we must agree that the surveyors or 3,500 years ago knew their job. At the end of that distance the Avenue split into two branches, as I have said earlier, one branch going toward the Cursus and the other toward Amesbury, after describing a curve northward.

The first branch is now placed in question, although it was reported in 1740 by Stukeley, who was a good observer, and later recognized by Colt Hoare in 1812 and Petrie in 1880. It is also said to have been identified in aerial photographs taken in 1921, but it is not indicated on the One-Inch Map of England & Wales No. 167—Salisbury. It is hard to verify in the present state of the terrain. The Cursus and the Avenue apparently date from different times.

In the middle of the eighteenth century the Avenue was thought to have been bordered by stones erected on the banks. No trace of such stones has been found, and the idea is now completely abandoned. It was probably based on the group of stones between the Sarsen Circle and the Heel Stone, including the Slaughter Stone.

The purpose of that impressive roadway is not known. Was it a ritual path for processions moving toward the point at which the sun rose at the summer solstice? This view was accepted for a time, but there are several facts against it. It is certain that the Avenue was not completely clear, at least at the end at which it joined the monument. Besides the Heel Stone and its little circular ditch, set almost in the middle of the Avenue, two holes that were undoubtedly used for holding stones have been found exactly on its axis. (They are marked B and C in Figure 4.) Furthermore, the ditch and bank partially cut across it.

There are also four post holes (A in Figure 4) in a straight line, before the Heel Stone and a little to the left of it. Since they are about 3 feet wide and 4 feet deep, they were meant for very large posts. They are older than the Avenue but may have been related to the henge monument. A line passing through its center and the center of the entrance is perpendicular to the line formed by the post holes. Judging from plans in which they are shown, the line formed by them apparently extends toward the point of sunrise at the winter solstice.

It thus seems unlikely that the Avenue was a kind of "sacred way." That it is partially blocked by the ditch and bank, the Aubrey Holes, and the small ditch around the Heel Stone shows that at one time the builders had little concern for it.

Another hypothesis, apparently more acceptable, is that the Avenue was the roadway on which stones used for building the monument were transported. According to Atkinson, it goes to the Avon, near Amesbury, where it has a width of about a hundred feet. It is likely that some of the stones were transported by waterways. Moreover, the path of the Avenue offers the best average slope, following contour lines as closely as possible. And finally, its origin at the Avon is not far from "Vespasian's Camp."

The camp is to the right of the road going from Amesbury to Stonehenge. It is also known as "the Ramparts." The name of "Vespasian's Camp" was given to it by Stukeley. It bears no resemblance to a Roman camp; instead, it suggests one of the ancient enclosures that are very numerous on Salisbury Plain. It is remarkable for its area (about 37 acres), the steepness of its edges, especially on the west side, and the fact that it touches the Avon on the southeast, which gave its occupants access to water. It is the prehistoric camp closest to Stonehenge and may have served as a shelter or dwelling for the many workers who built the structure. To the best of my knowledge, the site has not been extensively excavated.

To return to the Avenue, there is nothing to prevent us from assuming that it may have been both a processional way, at least for a certain time after its construction, and a road used for transporting stones, when the decision to build the main structure of Stonehenge had been made.

The Axis

The Axis brings us to one of the difficult points of Stonehenge: the axis of symmetry to which I have already referred several times. It is often mentioned in the literature of Stonehenge. British authors define it as an imaginary line passing through the middle of the spaces between uprights 55 and 56 of the central trilithon and 1 and 30 of the Sarsen Circle. It extended to the left of the Heel Stone and exactly coincided with the axis of the Avenue. Some authors believe it must have passed through the middle of the space between uprights 15 and 16 of the Sarsen Circle.

Of the three intervals mentioned above, only 30–1 is known since stones 15 and 55 are no longer in their original places. There are thus only two elements for situating the Axis: the middle of interval 30–1 and the axis of the Avenue. That is enough to determine it if it really exists as described. After ascertaining the axial line of the Avenue, one can study its extension through the monument. That is what seems to have been done by the surveyors of the Ordnance Survey Department. Working with precision instruments, they were able to make a highly accurate study. The Axis can be laid out by means of the following elements:

1. The axial line of the Avenue.
2. A point 1 foot from the left side of the Heel Stone, or 6 feet from its peak.*

*Divergences among the British authors from whom I have taken this information also make it possible to accept the

3. The middle of the interval between uprights 1 and 30 in the Sarsen Circle.

4. A point 1 foot 6 inches from the right side of upright 56.

5. A point 2 feet 6 inches from the right side of stone 16.

On either side of Stonehenge it was found that the Axis extends to two prehistoric sites, the ancient camps of Sidbury Hill, 8 miles to the northeast, and Grovely Castle, 6 miles to the southwest.

Other lines for the Axis have been laid out, notably by Petrie, Barclay, and Lockyer. They differ only slightly from that of the Ordnance Survey Department, but the latter has prevailed.

Since the extension of the axis of the Avenue to the middle of the interval between uprights 1 and 30 seemed too remarkable not to have an important meaning, that axis and the monument's axis of symmetry were assumed to be the same. The monument and the Avenue were thus bound together in the same past and the same purpose by that simple straight line.

But the importance given to the Axis in the literature of Stonehenge comes from the fact that its azimuth, the angle it forms with the meridian, is 49°34′, which is within less than 1 degree (56 minutes, to be exact) of the present direction of sunrise on June 21. Since the Axis seemed to be the monument's axis of symmetry, it was thought to mark the point of sunrise at the summer solstice when the monument was built. The difference of 56 minutes could be attributed to the precession of the equinoxes, and it would then be possible to calculate an approximate date for the construction of Stonehenge—provided the Axis was an axis of symmetry. But it is not.

It can be defined exactly as a straight line that follows the longitudinal axis of the Avenue and extends to the

---

figures of 1 foot 3 inches and 5 feet 10 inches. The figures of 1 foot and 6 feet are better suited to drawing up a precise plan.

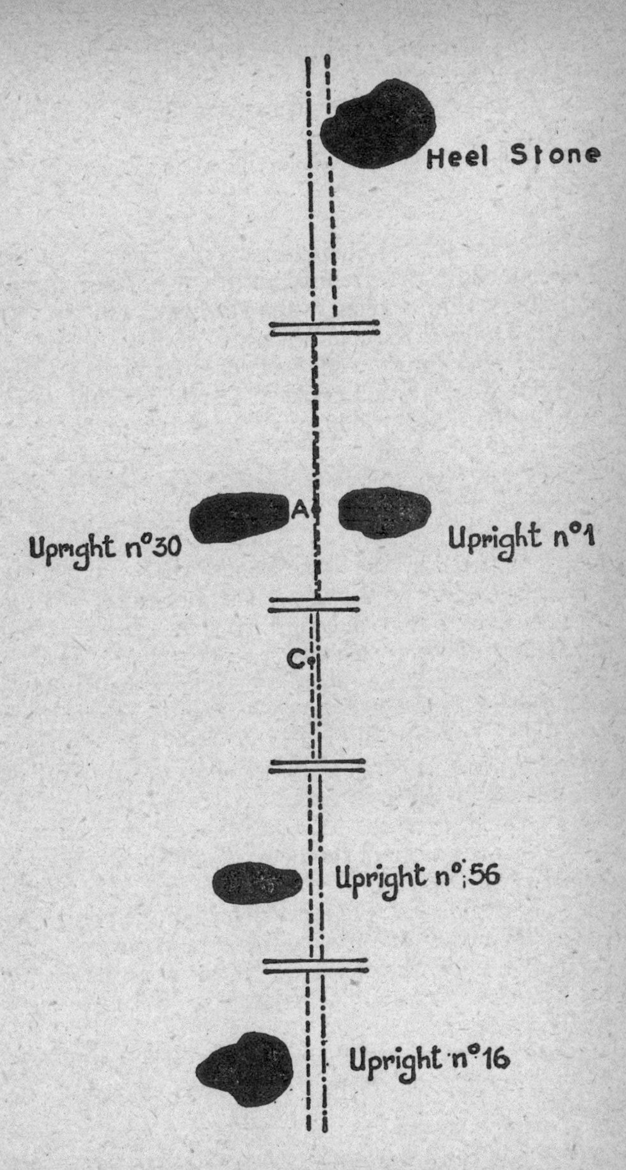

FIGURE 12—The Axis.

middle of the space between uprights 1 and 30 of the Sarsen Circle. That is all, because if we draw an axis of symmetry of the monument from the middle of that space, the two lines do not coincide. They are very close to each other, but if we are going to date something by a method based on astronomy, we are entitled to quibble over minute fractions of an inch.

First of all, the Axis does not pass through the center of the monument, which, it must be agreed, is a major defect for an axis of symmetry. And, as we have seen, it passes 1 foot 6 inches from upright 56 and 2 feet 6 inches from stone 16. This leads to attributing a length of 3 feet to the interval between the uprights of the Great Trilithon and 5 feet to the interval between uprights 15 and 16 of the Sarsen Circle, which is a foot and a half greater than the average interval between the stones of that circle.

I will therefore leave the Axis where it is, starting from the Sarsen Circle and extending along the Avenue, but before abandoning it to its fate, I will make one remark: The Avenue seems to be older than the monument. Is it simply a coincidence that the axis of the Avenue intersects the Sarsen Circle at such a remarkable point as the middle of interval 1–30? Certainly not. The builders of the monument must have been aware that the axis of the Avenue lies in the direction of sunrise at the summer solstice. When they aligned the monument in the same direction, they saw the divergence of the two orientations. The two lines had to intersect somewhere. The builders chose the middle of interval 1–30, which was probably an important point in the plan of the structure.

I will end this section on a curious note. In discussing the function of the Axis in the orientation of Stonehenge, some authors are convinced that the point for observing sunrise was just behind the Great Trilithon, with the observer standing on the ground. But in their plans of the restored monument they always place stone 67 in front of that observation point, on the Axis. Stone 67, now lying on the ground, had a height of 8 feet, making it the highest stone in the Bluestone Horseshoe, yet these authors place it directly in front of their observation point as blithely as if it were transparent!

The Horizon of Stonehenge

To complete my description, I must say something about what is sometimes called the "horizon of Stonehenge." I will do it briefly since at this point my goal is not to sum up the prehistory of Wiltshire, or even Salisbury Plain. A simple study of the prehistoric remains in that region would take hundreds of pages. I would have to speak, among other things, of the Neolithic or more recent camps or enclosures in the style of "Vespasian's Camp." One of the most outstanding is Ogbury Camp, on the left bank of the Avon about 2 miles south of Amesbury. It had an area of 6 acres and an entrance on its east side, cut into its ditch and bank.

I have already mentioned two other camps, Sidbury Hill and Grovely Castle. They are on opposite sides of Stonehenge, on the extension of the Axis. Should we attach any importance to that fact? I do not think so. First of all, I can see no purpose in such an alignment, although I must recognize that we know nothing about the mentality of Neolithic man. Furthermore, the two camps seem to date from the Iron Age, a period more recent than that of the monument. Their sites might have been chosen, however, by prolonging the Axis. Finally, I have ascertained other alignments of the same kind that, after study, turn out to be mere coincidences. There is nothing surprising about that since prehistoric remains are so numerous on Salisbury Plain. In any case, the fact has nothing to do with the Stonehenge monument, whose builders seem to have treated the Avenue and its axis with a certain offhandedness. I will conclude on this point by quoting Atkinson: "The chosen line [Grovely-Axis of Stonehenge-Sidbury Hill] has just as much, but no more, significance than the fact that the same line, if prolonged, passes through Copenhagen."

Another special feature of Salisbury Plain is the number of burial mounds that rise from its surface. As I have said, they are of two kinds, known as long barrows and round barrows. There are only about a dozen of the first kind but hundreds of the second. Within a 2-mile radius of Stonehenge more than 350 round barrows have been found. They are differentiated by their shapes and called bowl barrows, disk barrows, bell barrows, and so on. They often appear in clusters, as though tribes or families had separate burial areas. The long and round barrows date from different periods. The concentration of round barrows around Stonehenge is the largest in Great Britain, and probably the largest in Western Europe. Because of their extraordinary number and the richness of the furnishings found in some of them, the building of Stonehenge is generally attributed to the "round barrow people." But that people must have supplied only the labor, the concept of the monument having come from elsewhere.

One of the oldest and most curious monuments around Stonehenge is Woodhenge. It is often mentioned with its more impressive neighbor; some brochures, for example, bear the title "Stonehenge and Woodhenge." But that is about the same as associating the Cathedral of Notre-Dame in Paris with an ordinary village church.

Woodhenge is north of Amesbury, on the road to Marlborough. It is composed of six concentric series of holes, each series describing an ellipse with low eccentricity. The outermost one has a length of about 160 feet and a width of about 130. The number of holes in each ellipse is as follows, starting with the outermost and going inward: 60, 32, 16, 18, 18, 12. A grave was discovered in the middle of the monument. It contained the skeleton of a 3-year-old child whose skull had been split, perhaps in a propitiatory sacrifice.

If we imagine Woodhenge as it must have been, we do not have an idea of anything very impressive. Its holes are so numerous that its plan cannot be discerned at the site; its real nature appears only in a drawing. If each of those holes originally held a post, the overall effect must have been that of a clump of trees whose branches had been cut off—unless the posts supported

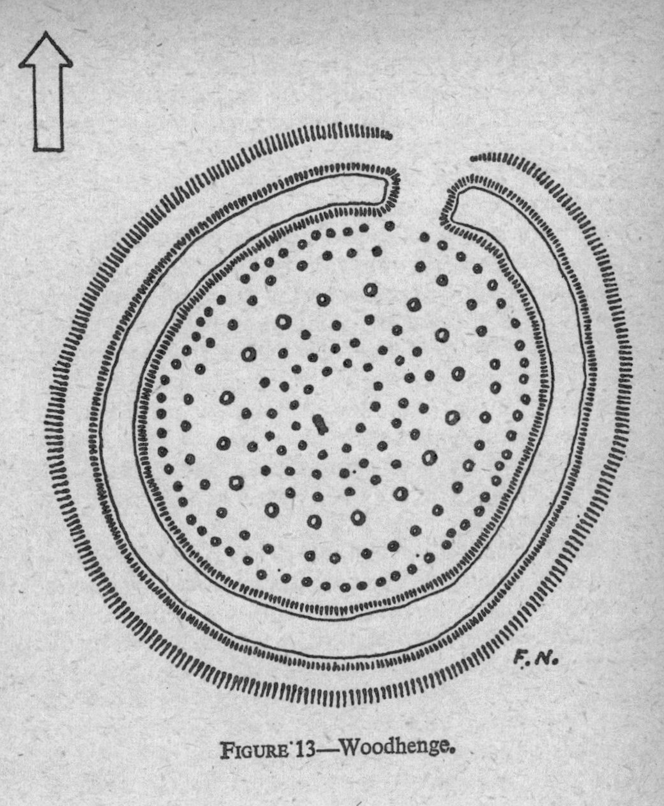

FIGURE 13—Woodhenge.

a roof. This seems quite possible, judging from the size of the holes in the third ellipse from the outside. The large posts in them may have supported the ridgepoles of a two-pitched roof that rested on the smaller posts in the other ellipses. The middle of the structure may have been open at the top, but even in that case the number of posts was greater than necessary.

Woodhenge has sometimes been regarded as a kind of wooden prototype of Stonehenge. It has been thought, in particular, that it may have embodied the system by which the sarsen lintels are assembled. I do not see how, and there is nothing to support such an assumption. Perhaps purlins connecting the tops of the posts in a single curve were assembled with V-shaped joints, but there is no evidence that this system was used with two tenons and two mortises at the top of a post. Only large ridgepoles resting on thick timbers could have connected the two systems. We cannot speak of girders in the modern sense of the word since the posts were not placed on a single radius.

But even if the system of joining the sarsen lintels had been used in Woodhenge, the two monuments would still not be comparable. Woodhenge would have looked like a huge storage hut, not a temple. A vaguely elliptical shape, a structure with more than 150 uprights in a relatively small space, the irregularity of the curves described by the holes, a wide ditch bordered by a bank —everything combines to make Woodhenge a monument that is quite distinctive but completely different from its overwhelming neighbor. And as though to accentuate the contrast, the post holes have been marked with concrete cylinders about 2 feet high. The effect is unfortunate. From a distance, it makes Woodhenge look like a storage area for fuel drums. Let us hope that no one will ever have the idea of doing the same thing with the Q, R, Y, and Z Holes of Stonehenge.

If we want to go back to Stonehenge from Woodhenge, we must first cross a large part of the Larkhill military base, then go down into a shallow depression in which we will be surprised if someone tells us that we are crossing one of the largest known Neolithic enclosures. It is the famous Cursus, shown on all maps of the Stonehenge area but hard to discern today. A layman to whom it is pointed out for the first time is likely to conclude that archaeology is a highly conjectural science. The Cursus was a simple earthwork marked by a ditch and bank about 1.7 miles long and 300 feet wide. It is oriented in an approximately east-west direction, with a difference of about 7 degrees. At its east end is a long barrow; the two round barrows that were once at its west end have been destroyed by the army. The idea that the Cursus may have been used as a course for chariot races has been seriously stated.

Finally, I will mention a curiosity. Not far to the northeast of Stonehenge, in the direction of Durrington and Bulford, there are isolated sarsen stones. How or why they came to be there, no one knows. There are at least three of them, and they were apparently reported for the first time by Stukeley. They are all small, or at least smaller than those used in the construction of Stonehenge. They constitute a little enigma because they are not on the route that was probably followed in transporting the other stones, yet they seem too heavy to have been brought from such a long distance if they came from the breaking up of some of the Stonehenge uprights; it would surely have been more sensible to break them into lighter pieces.

One of them is immersed in the Avon, a few inches under water, near Bulford. On its upper surface is an iron ring and a square hole about 1 foot wide and 5 inches deep. It is thought to have been used to support one of the piers of a footbridge.

The reader who has followed me this far, referring to the illustrations, is now acquainted with Stonehenge. I do not think I have omitted anything essential. If I have neglected a few details, they are of minor importance. Furthermore, we will return to many points, and we will have new insights resulting from discoveries made by British scientists.

PART TWO

The History of Stonehenge

The Builders of Stonehenge

It began in about 2300 B.C. At that time, in southern England and many other regions of Western Europe, there were people whose equivalent could perhaps be found in our own time among the Australian aborigines. They lived in precarious shelters made of branches and used bone harpoons and fishhooks, flint arrowheads and polished stone axes. They wore clothes made of animal skins and made extensive use of deer antlers for weapons and tools. They got their food by hunting, fishing, and gathering wild fruit. They lived from day to day, unable to store up supplies for times when they were deprived of food by scarcity of game, forest fires, or droughts. But in about 2300 B.C. newcomers landed on the south shore of England. From the continent, they brought a revolutionary way of life: They practiced farming and herding.

These newcomers first settled on the shores of the English Channel, then gradually began moving inland. They did not know metals, but they cleared the forests, and although they also hunted and fished, they lived mainly by herding and rudimentary farming. To some extent they were free from worry about what the next day would bring, and they had a little time to think.

We know these people, or at least the traces they left in Great Britain, under the name of the Windmill Hill Culture.

Windmill Hill is a Neolithic camp about a mile and a half northeast of Avebury and 18 miles north of Stonehenge. It is composed of three concentric ditches, each bordered by a bank, at least in the part that is still visible. The largest ditch enclosed an area of about 20 acres. Windmill Hill is a typical "causewayed camp," a term used in England to designate camps with an entrance gap, a kind of "bridge," in the surrounding earthwork. The nearest one to Stonehenge is Robin Hood Ball, 4 miles to the north.

The tools of the Windmill Hill Culture were still rudimentary. They consisted mainly of chipped flint scrapers, polished stone axes, antler picks like those found at Stonehenge, finely worked flint arrowheads, bone needles, and rather crude pottery, usually hemispherical in shape, sometimes with decorations composed of dotted lines or narrow vertical incisions. The people probably wore leather clothes, and besides their herd animals, they had domesticated the dog. They seem to have practiced cannibalism, probably for ritual or cultural purposes. Perhaps in a few special cases they also performed human sacrifices, as may be indicated by a grave containing the skeleton of a dwarf found in one of the ditches of Windmill Hill. The sacrifice of such an unusual person must have been pleasing to the gods. The camps do not seem to have been used as permanent dwellings. They must have been cattle enclosures or temporary refuges.

The Windmill Hill people are especially known as those who made the long barrows. Many of those mounds are more than 100 feet long, and some are more than 330 feet long. By the amount of work they represent, such monuments imply a society organized into groups larger than the family. The earth that covers the long barrows was obtained by digging trenches along the side, following the same principle used in making the banks of the camps and henge monuments.

The mounds often have an east-west orientation, the east end higher than the west. The bodies buried in them were usually placed in the higher end.

There are about a hundred long barrows in Wiltshire, including ten within a 2-mile radius of Stonehenge. The nearest one is a few dozen yards away, to the left of the road to Warminster. Another one lies to the southwest, at Normanton Down, and I have already mentioned the one at the east end of the Cursus. The Cursus may have been related to the long barrow, and consequently both may have been made by the same people. It is generally believed, however, that the Cursus is more recent.

We have no proof that the Windmill Hill people took part in the construction of a primitive phase of Stonehenge. But the concentration of long barrows and earthworks of the Cursus type around the monument is considered sufficient to show that the tribes of that people regarded the region with a certain interest or special veneration.

In the course of the excavations carried out in 1958, a fragment of Windmill Hill pottery was found in a trench that may have been the inclined plane used for erecting the Heel Stone. To the best of my knowledge, it is the oldest vestige so far found at the site of Stonehenge. But even though excavations in henge monuments have uncovered similar fragments, this vestige unfortunately does not seem enough to justify concluding that the Heel Stone was erected by the Windmill Hill people. There is nothing to preclude that idea, however.

The Windmill Hill Culture was eventually supplanted by that of the megalithic monument builders, which continued for several centuries and covered all of Western Europe with its strange monuments. One curious case is the long barrow of the West Kennet Avenue, southwest of Avebury, in which a handsome dolmen with lateral chambers is buried. It is reminiscent of the great mound and dolmen of Mané-Lud, at

Locmariaquer, in the Morbihan department of France, except for the division into lateral chambers.

One of the most impressive achievements of the megalithic culture is the gigantic Avebury cromlech, with a diameter of nearly 1,000 feet. It is surrounded by a deep ditch and a bank. There were two other circles of standing stones inside it. The eastern part is rather well preserved, but there are hardly any stones left in the western part. All the menhirs in the monument are sarsens from nearby outcrops. The identical quality of the stones is the only common point between Avebury and Stonehenge. I would add the circular shape if the great circle of Avebury were not hopelessly irregular.

Many of the menhirs in the cromlech are diamond-shaped, with one of their points sunk into the ground, which gives them an odd appearance. In the western part of the circle, the missing stones have been replaced with small concrete pyramids. Many British authors believe that Avebury was built by the Beaker people, whom we will discuss later, and not by the Windmill Hill people or those who made the megalithic structures. The monument may have been built in several phases. Avebury has also had the honor of being associated with Stonehenge in many books. Above all, I believe, it deserves to be placed at the top of the list of all the world's circular cromlechs.

Aside from their impressive structures, the builders of the megalithic monuments left nothing that differentiates them from other populations. In England, the idea of erecting monuments of the dolmen and menhir types probably came from the continent (though this cannot be stated with certainty), but we do not know if it was brought by individuals or by tribes whose way of life was the same as that of the native peoples. Be that as it may, one important element appears in the construction of these monuments: the knowledge required for lifting and transporting heavy masses. That knowledge included, at least, use of the lever, the inclined plane, transport by means of rollers, and a few rudiments of astronomy and geometry. Serious study of what remains of the megaliths above ground leads to the conclusion that their builders, or at least some of them, knew how to lay out a circle and a right angle, divide an angle into two equal parts, and orient their monuments toward outstanding positions of the sun.

Within three or four centuries after the arrival of the Windmill Hill people, fusion with the original populations had been accomplished. There were then only two distinct kinds of peoples, one still living in the Mesolithic stage, the other within the framework of the Neolithic culture that had been brought from the continent. The first was gradually absorbed, and from that fusion was born what British specialists call the Secondary Neolithic.

The people of that period were hunters and fishermen like those of the Mesolithic and farmers and herders like the Windmill Hill people. But with them, new activities appeared in Great Britain, activities that might almost be called commerce and industry. They exploited flint mines and outcrops of igneous rocks, made axes and transported them over considerable distances to exchange them for other objects. Four axes made of polished green stone from an outcrop near Marazion, in Cornwall, have been found inside Stonehenge.

There are very few traces of permanent dwellings dating from the Secondary Neolithic. The same is true of that whole general period when the dwellings of the dead seem to have been more comfortable, or at least more durable, than those of the living. One might conclude that in spite of agriculture those people were nomads or seminomads. But a special kind of structure is attributed to them, the kind known as henge monuments.

They were neither cattle enclosures nor shelters from enemy attacks. They are generally thought to have been temples or sanctuaries, and they are peculiar to Great Britain. Their sizes vary greatly, but they are usually circular in shape, with one or two entrances. I have already spoken of them. The smallest one is at Fargo Plantation, near Stonehenge, with a diameter of only 26 feet. One of the largest, Durrington Walls, near Woodhenge, has a diameter of more than 1,400 feet. The road from Amesbury to Marlborough goes through the middle of it.

One kind of henge monument has a circle of holes inside its bank. I believe that circle is later than the earthwork because some of the holes are often dug in the entrances. That is the case in Stonehenge, where the Aubrey Holes are spaced at regular intervals without taking account of the gaps in the ditch and bank.

The people of the Secondary Neolithic may thus have made the ditch, bank, and Aubrey Holes, constituting an early stage of Stonehenge. Woodhenge, Durrington Walls, and the Cursus are considered to be in the same category as this monument. The regularity of the Aubrey Holes allows us to assume that the people who made them knew how to lay out very large circles on the ground. The technique had probably been brought by those who oversaw construction of the megalithic monuments. The original phase of Stonehenge might thus be regarded as a kind of prototype of the henge monuments if only because of the perfection of its layout, provided it could be demonstrated that it once contained a stone or wooden structure.

The henge monuments are far from all being the same. Some have only a circular ditch and bank, with no holes; others had wooden posts arranged in a circle, an ellipse or some other shape. That is why many authors have believed that a wooden structure in the style of Woodhenge, though not as large, may have existed inside Stonehenge. In monuments of this kind, in which the bank was wholly or partially lined with holes, the holes are always associated with charred remains.

Finally, according to British archaeologists, the people of the Secondary Neolithic must be credited with a remarkable feat: transporting the 35-ton block of the Heel Stone from the Marlborough Downs and then

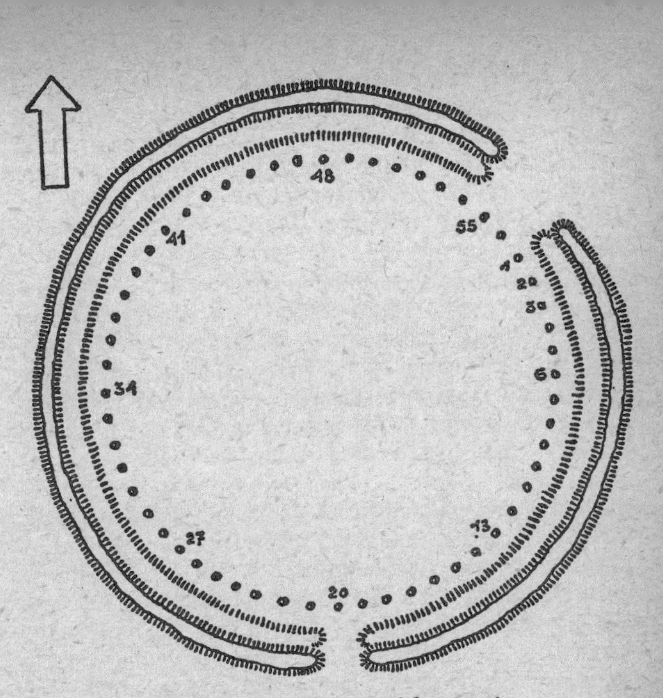

FIGURE 14—The Henge Monument

erecting it. That is not a record, but it is still impressive.

Shortly after completion of that part of Stonehenge in about 1700 B.C., many colonists landed on the shores of the English Channel and the North Sea. They are known as the Beaker people, from the most characteristic object of their material culture: baked clay containers 6 to 8 inches high, with a capacity of 2 or 3 pints, decorated with geometrical designs on a large part of their outer surface. Because of their shape, they are sometimes called bell beakers.

The Beaker people are thought to have come from the Rhineland, although their origin seems to have been in the Iberian Peninsula. In the Rhineland they may have been influenced by contact with the Battle-

Axe people, who came from the east and had axes or war clubs consisting of a wooden handle fitted into a perforated stone head.

We know little about the everyday life of the Beaker people; most of our knowledge of them comes from their graves. But with them came several important innovations. Collective graves—the long barrows of the Windmill Hill and Secondary Neolithic peoples—were replaced by individual graves: the round barrows. Then came knowledge and use, if not manufacture, of copper and gold objects. In this period, 1700 to 1600 B.C., there was a great center for the manufacture and distribution of copper, then bronze, in Ireland.

Trade routes over land and sea were probably established between Ireland and southern England in those remote times. But even if metal was traded on the west coast of Wales, there was still contact with the seagoing people who brought it. It was no doubt through these commercial exchanges that the Beaker people living in Wessex learned of the wondrous virtues of certain stones found somewhere in the faraway west.

The objects, especially battle axes, found in the round barrows of that period reveal a warlike society. Those individual graves also give evidence of a certain aristocracy in a society in which differences of condition were more sharply marked than among the preceding peoples.

A new kind of religious monument first appeared in that period: the circle of stones inside the henge monument. The impressive Avebury cromlech is a typical example. It was evidently made by the Beaker people since some handsome bell beakers were buried in graves near the menhir-lined Kennet Avenue.

But apparently something new came into the lives of the Beaker people on Salisbury Plain, something that remains inexplicable in the present state of our knowledge. At the site of Stonehenge, they should logically have left a circle of untooled stones, as at Avebury, approximately on the circle of the Aubrey Holes. And those stones should have been taken from the nearest source, somewhere in the vicinity of Marlborough, let us say.* That would be in conformity with what prehistory teaches us.

Instead, what do we find? A cromlech, yes, but a cromlech of a special kind that can be called unique. Although the double circle of bluestones may be the work of the Beaker people, it is the only one of its kind, to the best of my knowledge. I am speaking only of its design, of course, since its construction was never finished. (See Figure 10.) It does not consist of two concentric circles as in the Avebury sanctuary but of a double circle since the stones were to be placed in pairs on a single radius. An entrance or an orientation marked by rows of several stones would also have been a unique detail in the circles of untooled stones. Finally, the choice of materials is extraordinary because it led the builders to break all known records in the ancient world for transporting heavy materials over long distances. We will return to that amazing feat later.

Commerce has always been a source of wealth. This truth was already apparent to the peoples living in Wiltshire in about 1500 B.C. Why did Salisbury Plain become such an important commercial center at that time? Its geographical situation was undoubtedly one of the main reasons. As we have seen, it is at the point where the downs converge, and those lines were usually followed by the prehistoric roads known as ridgeways, which made it possible to avoid streams. One of the most important of those roads ran in a northeast-southwest direction from Dorset to Norfolk without crossing any streams but the Little Ouse and the Thames. Geography is a very old science.

By about 1400 B.C. we are in the presence of the Wessex Culture. That is what Professor Piggott, of Edinburgh, calls a phase of prehistoric life in southern

*Are the holes for stones on the circle of the Four Stations (F, G, K in Figure 4) vestiges of an ancient cromlech or an attempt to build one? I do not think so. They seem to have been meant for isolated stones.

England characterized mainly by the richness and variety of the furnishings found in one category of round barrows. Once again we know the people of the period only by their graves. Are we to conclude that they lived as nomads or seminomads? We might think so, although their dwellings might have been tents, like those of modern Bedouins.* In any case they lived in Wiltshire, as is shown by the number of their round barrows. Furthermore, the great sarsen structure is attributed to them. It required a great deal of time and large numbers of workers; it could not have been built by a few wandering tribes. For many years, thousands of people lived around Stonehenge. It is strange that only the graves of some of their leaders remain.

Where did the people of the Wessex Culture come from? The term is generally used to designate not a distinct people, like the Windmill Hill and Beaker peoples, but a kind of religious, martial, and commercial aristocracy. How was it formed? Probably by means of wealth acquired from trade or by a forcible seizure of power, or perhaps both. It has been thought that this aristocracy came from French Brittany and became dominant in Wessex through the superiority of its weapons.

Be that as it may, what we have is a minority that, by violence or other means, made a majority carry out an overwhelming task: transporting, shaping, and erecting the enormous sarsen blocks. But we must not think of this work too much in terms of Herodotus's description of how the Egyptian pyramids were built. Stonehenge may have been built under the impetus of a religious ideal. Moreover, the erection of the megalithic monuments shows that people of that time were accustomed to great works.

The round barrows of the Wessex Culture are surrounded by a ditch and an outer bank. This represents, at least in appearance, a fusion of the Beaker people's

*In Caesar's time, the Britons' dwellings were made of reeds and wood (Diodorus Siculus, V, 21). If they were the same a thousand years earlier, as they probably were, it is not surprising that nothing remains of them.

mounds and the henge monuments of the Secondary Neolithic. Some barrows are bell-shaped, rather high, and occupy all the space inside the ditch. Others are of insignificant height, and the overall effect is of a small henge monument without an opening. Between these two kinds, bell barrows and disk barrows, are a certain number of intermediate types. The first are generally graves of men, while the second seem to have been meant for women.

In the furnishings, besides perforated stone battle axes, there are bronze tools and swords whose hilt guards are richly adorned with gold. The bronze axes seem to have come from southern Bohemia. There are also necklaces made of amber beads that came from southern Europe and not from Scandinavia. Among the most surprising exotic objects are small, blue faience beads whose bright color has been dulled by time. Close examination of them has shown that they were made in Egypt. The presence of such objects in Crete and on the Atlantic coasts of Spain and France suggests that they were imported by sea.

It is thus not impossible that the people of the Wessex Culture were not only acquainted with eastern Mediterranean civilizations but also had contact with them. In Egypt during that period, Thutmose III succeeded Queen Hatshepsut, who had organized long-distance commercial expeditions. The Phoenicians had perhaps sailed beyond the Pillars of Hercules. The great Minoan empire was flourishing in Crete, and in Mycenae there were domed tombs whose style is found in Western Europe, for example, in the famous megalithic monument of New Grange, near Droghedda, Ireland. Later, in a curious and unexpected way, we will find another piece of supporting evidence for the possibility of relations between Mediterranean civilizations and the people of the Wessex Culture.

Diodorus Siculus

By about 1300 B.C., Stonehenge had taken on its final form. How long was it used as a temple? We cannot say, but there is a passage in Diodorus Siculus that is often quoted and debated. Diodorus, a Greek historian born at Agyrium, Sicily, was a contemporary of Caesar and Augustus. He lived in Rome a long time and worked thirty years on his *Historical Library,* in forty books, of which long fragments are extant. Although he did not have a critical mind, according to some, he left us some valuable information drawn from ancient works that have now completely disappeared. Here is the famous passage from his *Historical Library:*

> Since we have come to speak of the northern lands of Asia, it will not be inappropriate to say a few words about the Hyperboreans. Among the historians who have recorded the traditions of Antiquity in their annals, Hecataeus and a few others maintain that beyond Transalpine Gaul, in the ocean, there is an island as large as Sicily. This island, situated in the north, they say, is inhabited by the Hyperboreans, so named because they live beyond the point from which the boreal [north] wind blows. The soil of the island is excellent, and so remarkably fertile that it produces two crops a year.
>
> Here, according to the same story, is the birthplace of Leto, which explains why the islanders have a special veneration for Apollo. They are all, so to speak, priests of that god. Each day they sing hymns in his honor. On that island there is also a vast enclosure consecrated to Apollo, as well as a magnificent round temple adorned with numerous offerings. The islanders' city is also dedicated to Apollo. Most of its inhabitants are cithara players who, in the temple, constantly extol the god by accompanying the hymn-singing on their instruments.
>
> The Hyperboreans speak a language peculiar to them. They are very kindly disposed toward the Greeks, particularly the Athenians and Delians, and these feelings go back to a very ancient past. It is said that several Greeks have come to visit

Inside view.
Trilithon 53-54.
(Author's collection.)

The lintel of the Great Trilithon, with its mortises. *(Author's collection.)*

Trilithon lintel, showing the special shape designed
to attenuate the effects of perspective. *(Author's collection.)*

Tenon on the top of stone 56. It fitted into the
right-hand hole of the lintel shown on the opposite page.
(Salisbury Museum. Photo R.J.C. Atkinson.)

Overall view of the temple. *(Photo Aerofilms Ltd.)*

Stone 68 with its longitudinal groove, upright 56 of the central trilithon, and restored trilithon 58-58. *(Author's collection.)*

Stele found at Mycenae. *(Athens National Museum. Author's collection.)*

The dagger carved on upright 54. *(Author's collection.)*

Fallen upright 59, showing traces of preliminary dressing. *(Author's collection.)*

Restored trilithon 57-58. *(Author's collection.)*

Hoc tempore sanctus Paulinus
romanus civis
[illegible] qui pro [illegible] filio
vidue se tradidit [illegible]
[illegible] de quo scribit beatus
Gregorius in dialogo suo.

Sanctus [illegible]
[illegible] fortis sanctus [illegible]
[illegible]
Iste zenoni [illegible] nos
[illegible] a [illegible]
[illegible] xvi.

Huius tempore passa est [illegible]

[illegible]

Aurelius Ambrosius

Iste cum [illegible]
[illegible] filius con
[illegible]
[illegible]

[illegible]

[illegible] apud Stanhenges

[illegible]

Tempore Gelasii pape inventum
corpus beati Barnabe apostoli et
evangelium quod ipsius manu
scriptum [illegible]

Iste anastasius
imperavit annis xxvii.

Huius tempore [illegible]
[illegible] inventum
[illegible]
[illegible]
[illegible]

Huius tempore floruerunt isti sancti

Sanctus Dubricius

[illegible]

[illegible]

Arnulphus

Maxentius

Leodegarius

Iste [illegible]

Inside view of the Sarsen Circle, with the Heel Stone in the background. *(Author's collection.)*

Stonehenge, according to a fourteenth-century manuscript. *(Corpus Christi College, Cambridge.)*

Sunrise on June 21, seen from the center of the monument.
(Photo Georg Gerster—Rapho.)

The Heel Stone, seen in profile. *(Author's collection.)*

The Stonehenge temple. *(Photo Aerofilms Ltd.)*

Outside view of the Sarsen Circle. *(Author's collection.)*

Inside view, with trilithon 53-54 on the left.
(Author's collection.)

the Hyperboreans and left offerings bearing Greek inscriptions, and that, reciprocally, Abaris the Hyperborean once traveled in Greece to renew with the Delians the friendship existing between the two peoples.

It is also said that the moon, seen from that island, appears to be very close to the earth, and that risings of the ground can be distinctly observed there. Apollo is said to come down to the island every nineteen years. It is also at the end of that period that the heavenly bodies return to their point of departure after their revolution. That period of nineteen years is known to the Greeks as the Great Year. Every night during his appearance, from the vernal equinox to the rising of the Pleiades, the god dances, accompanying himself on the cithara, as though to enjoy the honors rendered to him.

Kings called Boreades, descendants and successors of Boreas, rule the island and provide for maintenance of its temple.

It is generally agreed that when Diodorus Siculus speaks of a magnificent round temple on an island in the ocean, he may be referring to Stonehenge. Unfortunately, this text is like many others that can be interpreted in different ways because the author is not explicit enough. That is why it has also been regarded as a fable with no scientific validity. I will not discuss the arguments pro and con. Diodorus, or the authors he summarized, tended to present the island of the Hyperboreans as a kind of paradise, and that may seem rather childish. It would be hard to recognize Salisbury Plain by that description, even with a favorable bias. And it would be equally hard to take seriously the two crops a year, the moon closer to the earth, the constant cithara playing, the city consecrated to Apollo, and so on. But we should always be cautious with legends.

It also seems clear that the text contains a few truths. All fantastic stories have some basis in reality, however slight. For the authors summarized by Diodorus, a large northern island beyond Transalpine Gaul was a piece of accurate information. It was surely England, although a peninsula like Jutland or Scandinavia has also been considered. After all, if Avebury and Stonehenge did not exist, the vast enclosure and the magnificent round temple dedicated to Apollo might also be regarded as imaginary. Those are two specific, verifiable assertions that seem to be based on something more than fable because, except for Avebury and Stonehenge, no trace of a vast enclosure and a circular temple on an island or a peninsula in the ocean has ever been found anywhere from the Ural Mountains to Ireland.

I will add something that, though less specific, may someday be confirmed: relations between the Greeks of the heroic period and the Hyperboreans of the large island. Finally, there is a detail that seems important to me: the reference to the rising of the Pleiades. In ancient times the Pleiades were the sailor's constellation since the most favorable period for sea travel was between its rising and its setting, that is, from May to November.

As for the Hecataeus mentioned by Diodorus Siculus, several ancient authors bore that name. In this case he was probably referring to Hecataeus of Abdera, a Greek geographer of the fourth century B.C. who wrote a book on the Hyperboreans. Judging from the text quoted above, he was not the only one who had heard of the marvelous temple on a large island in the ocean. There is nothing surprising in that. By its contrast with its surroundings, Stonehenge must have made a deep impression on everyone who saw it intact. The traders of the ancient world seem to have been great travelers, more intrepid in any case than historians and geographers. They may have spoken about Stonehenge in the eastern Mediterranean basin. If so, the temple was apparently still in use seven or eight hundred years before Christ.

The Destruction of Stonehenge

The present ruined state of Stonehenge has always suggested deliberate human action. Two periods have been proposed for the destruction: the Roman occupation and the Middle Ages. It is easy to imagine why it might have occurred in the Middle Ages. Not only in England but all over Europe, the people had great veneration for old stones, up to the eighteenth or nineteenth century, in some cases. The church was probably responsible for the destruction of many megalithic monuments from the fifth century onward. It is surprising, in fact, that so many still remain. But such an operation would have been uncharacteristic of the Romans, and there is little reason to attribute it to them.

Those who are inclined to believe in a destruction during the Roman occupation base their view on the large number of stone chips that enter into the composition of Stonehenge and are found at a level more or less corresponding to that period. All those fragments cannot be explained by the handling and transportation of the stones, although many may have come from the process of shaping them. Furthermore, it is said, the Romans may have feared that Stonehenge would become the symbol of a certain nationalism and a dangerous center of rebellion against the occupying power.

First of all, it seems unlikely that Roman soldiers would have bothered to break the sarsens or bluestones into little fragments. If they wanted to destroy the monument, they had only to topple the uprights. Who, at that time, would have erected them again? And when Caesar came to England, the Beaker people and the Wessex Culture had long since been supplanted by the Celts. It is doubtful that the Celts would have intended to create a center of rebellion at Stonehenge. Had Stonehenge become a Druidic temple?

In support of the idea that the ruined state of the monument must be attributed to human action, Stonehenge has been compared with Avebury. It has been pointed out that, at Avebury, stones sunk much less deeply into the ground than at Stonehenge are still standing. That is true, but let us examine things more closely. If, in Figure 3, we draw a north-south line a little to the left of the center of the monument, it divides

Stonehenge into clearly differentiated parts. In the western part, we find less than a dozen stones still upright, while the other part has twenty-four. And this latter part, with eleven successive uprights in the Sarsen Circle and two trilithons intact, shows a continuity lacking in the western part, where the stones still in place are isolated. The western side of the monument is more exposed to the sometimes violent winds that blow across Salisbury Plain.

Is the wind a sufficient cause for such destruction? Yes, or at least partially. It is related to the location of the monument: on an immense high plateau, with no protecting hills. Also, the size and shape of the stones favored the action of the wind. The rectangular shape given to them transformed them into screens offering an ideal surface to the pressure of the wind. The same is generally not true of unfashioned stones. There is no need to use aerodynamic formulas to show that a factory chimney will resist wind better than a screen of the same height and width. Some menhirs with shapes similar to that of the Stonehenge uprights are now leaning or lying on the ground in the opposite direction from the prevailing winds.

Taking the average area of an upright in the Sarsen Circle, not counting the lintel, as 90,000 square feet, a wind blowing 20 miles per hour will exert a pressure of about 150 pounds on it. But as the speed of the wind rises, the pressure increases drastically. It is close to 1,000 pounds for a wind of 45 miles per hour, which is relatively common, and in a severe windstorm it may go beyond 3,000 pounds. And we are here considering an isolated upright. If we take the Great Trilithon in its entirety, the pressures given above become 550, 3,300 and 13,000 pounds!

They are calculated for a surface directly facing the wind. This is not the case with all the uprights, but the resulting decrease in pressure is partly offset by the discontinuity of the wind's effort and the fact that the uprights stand precariously in their holes because of the inclined plane that was dug into each hole to facilitate sliding in the stone and then erecting it. And some uprights are not set deeply enough into the ground. This would not have happened in an ordinary cromlech, in which the stones could be of different heights. At Stonehenge, a shorter stone had to be buried at a smaller depth since the tops of all the uprights had to be at the same level.

The Great Trilithon is typical in this respect. I have already mentioned the imbalance created by the different depths at which its uprights are buried: 7 feet 7 inches for 56, 3 feet for 55. When trilithon 57–58 was set upright again in 1958, the workers were surprised to find that the foundation holes were so shallow that there were practically no inclined planes. It was hard to see how the trilithon had remained standing till modern times. The same remarks apply to certain stones in the Sarsen Circle. Judging from the lengths of those lying on the ground, some of them were buried at inadequate depths. Also, the lower ends of some stones are pointed, either naturally or not, which decreased their ability to withstand wind pressure.

It is therefore possible that natural forces played an important part in the destruction of Stonehenge. In the time since the monument began to be studied scientifically, several stones have fallen from natural causes. A few years ago some uprights were leaning dangerously and had to be secured by pouring concrete into their foundations. Some are still leaning.

Natural causes, however, must have been helped by human action. Many stones are missing, especially among the lintels of the Sarsen Circle. In a region as poor in building stone as Salisbury Plain, this is understandable, and it is surprising that more are not missing. Yet certain cases are hard to explain, whatever the cause of the fall or disappearance of the stones.

Let us take, for example, lintel 105, which joined uprights 5 and 6 of the Sarsen Circle. It has disappeared, but its neighbors, 104 and 106, are still in place. Its fall cannot be attributed to wind. But if it was removed by men, it is strange that one of its neighbors was not taken away first. With them in place, the operation was difficult, laborious and dangerous. Scaffoldings had to be built on each side of the uprights so that the lintel could be raised to disengage the tenons and V-shaped joints. Referring to Figure 8, the reader will see what a complicated task it was, especially with stones weighing 5 or 6 tons. Even breaking the lintel without first removing it would have involved useless extra work because breaking one of the lintels beside it would have made it easier to disengage. And the whole process would have been rather dangerous since even the fragments may have weighed 2 tons.

The case of trilithon 59–60 is equally puzzling. How was its enormous lintel removed from the tenons of the uprights? It is hard to explain because upright 60 is still in place, while 59 is on the ground. If the fall of 59 caused the fall of the lintel, 60 should have been strongly tilted, as in the Great Trilithon. The tenon prevented the lintel from sliding, and the fall of one upright caused the fall of the other. Furthermore, upright 60 was one of the most precarious because of the excavation that weakened its base, as I have mentioned earlier. And the fragments of the lintel are so far from the foot of the trilithon—the nearest one is 13 feet away, the farthest 25 feet—that they seem to have been hurled by some sort of supernatural force.

The destruction of this trilithon could conceivably have happened as follows: While one group of men pressed down on levers to disengage the lintel from the top of upright 60, another group toppled upright 59. But that would have been unnecessarily difficult since the whole trilithon could have been brought down by digging around its bases. I therefore prefer to think that upright 59 may have settled more deeply into the ground. If so, this caused one end of the lintel to sink until its increasing pressure on the upright caused it to fall. The small height of the tenon above upright 60 helped to free the lintel at that end, and in the fall of upright 59 it was thrown, as though by a sling, to the distance at which it now lies.

To sum up, it seems to me that the ruined state of Stonehenge must be largely attributed to natural causes and certain weaknesses in its foundations. To the best of my knowledge, Stonehenge is the only large monument in which the visible parts and the buried parts are homogeneous. That has its drawbacks. It is not certain, of course, that if the monument had not begun to collapse from natural causes, its destruction would not have been ordered by the church. At Avebury, the western part is better preserved than the eastern part, while the opposite is true at Stonehenge. This is because the menhirs on the western side of Avebury are sheltered from the wind by the bank, whereas those on the other side are not.

The only significant defect in the construction of Stonehenge was that inadequacy of its foundations. It did not result from ignorance on the part of the builders. They were aware of the problem, as is shown by the way they shaped the base of upright 55. They were probably unable to find enough stones with sufficient length; also, they had to respect certain proportions, which necessarily diminished the stability of the structure.

The Dance of the Giants

The first writer known to have mentioned Stonehenge is Henry of Huntingdon, author of *Historia Anglorum*, written in the second half of the eleventh century. Describing the wonders of Great Britain, he says, "The second one is at Stonehenge, where stones of amazing size are erected like porches, so that one door seems to have been placed on another.* It would be difficult to say by what means they were raised so high and why they were put in that place."

But in about the same period a Welsh writer adopted a more prudent attitude. Geoffrey of Monmouth (1100?–1154) wrote his *Historia Regum Britanniae* under the inspiration of ancient Celtic legends. In it he speaks of an episode which occurred in about the year 475, during the long struggle between the Saxons

*It may have been on the basis of Henry of Huntingdon's text that some people imagined a small trilithon perched on top of a larger one.

and the Britons. For centuries his story placed Stonehenge in the framework of a legend that was probably of Welsh origin. It happened during the reign of the Briton Vortigern, elected King of England in 445, after the departure of the Roman legions, during the long war he waged against the Saxons and particularly against Hengist, their king.

The two sides decided to make peace and agreed to hold a conference near Ambri (Amesbury). It was stipulated that the members of both sides were to come without weapons, but Hengist, who had sworn to overthrow the whole nobility of Britain, told his men to come to the conference with daggers hidden under their clothes. When he gave the signal, each Saxon was to kill the Briton beside him.

On the appointed day, the two groups met at a place thought to have been near Stonehenge, if not at Stonehenge itself. After the conference had begun, Hengist suddenly rushed at Vortigern and gave the signal. The Saxons took out their daggers and treacherously slaughtered the trusting, unarmed British noblemen. Thus, several hundred members of the local nobility were murdered, including Vortigern. The "betrayal of the long knives" is thought to have taken place in 461.

Vortigern was succeeded by Aurelius Ambrosius, a Roman who had been brought up in Britain. Wishing to commemorate the death of Vortigern and his companions, he decided to erect a monument on the site of the massacre.

That monument, according to Geoffrey of Monmouth, was none other than Stonehenge, and here is his version of how things happened. Since Aurelius Ambrosius wanted the monument to be imperishable, he called on Merlin the Enchanter for help. "Go to Killarus [Kildare], a mountain in Ireland," Merlin said to him, "and fetch the Dance of the Giants, great stones which possess wondrous qualities. If they can be placed here, in a circle on this ground, they will remain for all eternity."

"How can we bring such heavy stones from such a

great distance?" asked Ambrosius. "Have we no stones of equally good quality in our own land?"

"No," replied Merlin. "Those of the Dance of the Giants are sacred stones and they cure all ills. The Giants of bygone times brought them from the most distant shores of Africa, because of their virtues. When a Giant fell ill, his companions bathed him in water that had been used for washing the stones, and he was cured. The stones can also heal wounds if certain herbs are added."

Having heard this, the Britons resolved to go to Ireland and make war on the people there if they refused to part with the stones. They raised an army of fifteen thousand men and placed it under the command of Uther the Pendragon. Merlin went with them.

In Ireland they had to do battle against the young and valiant Gillomanius, who, when he saw the army of the Britons, cried out, "As long as I am alive, not one stone of the Dance of the Giants will leave Ireland!" But he was defeated and the Britons went to Killarus, where the sight of the stones filled them with wonder. When they tried to move them, however, their efforts proved to be futile. It was then that Merlin intervened. Solely by the effect of his magic power, the stones were lifted with incredible ease and transported to the ships. The Britons joyously set sail, and a good wind brought them back to England.

When Ambrosius learned of all this, he assembled the people and the clergy on Mount Ambrius. The stones of the Dance of the Giants were then erected, still under the guidance of Merlin, in the same arrangement they had had at Killarus. And Geoffrey of Monmouth concludes by saying that the part played by Merlin in the construction of Stonehenge proves the predominance of art over force.

A variant of this story was later given by the sixteenth-century English humanist John Leland in his *Commentaria de Scriptoribus Britannicis*. It is again Merlin who presides over the erection of the stones, but this time they have not come from Ireland. They have been taken from the environs of Salisbury Plain, and

Merlin's skill in the art of moving heavy stones is again stressed.

In the Middle Ages as in our time, Stonehenge appealed to the imagination, and it is only natural that it should have been attributed to King Arthur's famous counselor Merlin, Myrddhin in Welsh, one of the most popular figures of the period. He was the creator of the Order of the Round Table. Could this have been a reference to the table formed by the lintels of the Sarsen Circle? Stonehenge is to some extent related to the Arthurian cycle and the quest for the Holy Grail. King Arthur was the son of Uther the Pendragon, who commanded the army that went to Ireland for the stones of Stonehenge. Merlin helped Uther to win the favor of the fair Igerne, and Arthur was born of their union.

But who was Merlin? Did he really exist, or was he only a legendary figure spawned by the imagination of the Welsh bards? Robert de Boron presents him as a son of the devil, but it seems more plausible to me that he was a real man whose knowledge appeared supernatural, in those remote times, to the primitive people of southern England. He then passed into the pantheon of an imprecise mythology, along with the giants whose dance remained petrified in the great monoliths of Stonehenge.

As I have said before, we must always adopt a cautious attitude toward legends. It is a commonplace to say that they contain a particle of truth. In the legend of Merlin we see certain aspects of the real history of Stonehenge, notably the distant origin of the stones. If Geoffrey of Monmouth's story had been considered more attentively, there might have been fewer foolish hypotheses on that origin. I will also point out the idea of a master builder, with knowledge that was prodigious for his time, who presided over the construction of the monument. Who can doubt the existence of such a master, considering what remains of Stonehenge today?

We will probably never know the original name of Stonehenge, assuming it had one. Although it has no scientific basis, "The Dance of the Giants" seems appropriate for such an impressive monument, and it is easy to believe that it was one of the names used before the present one. At least some form of the word "giant" may have appeared in an earlier name. That would not be surprising since the word is found in many popular expressions used to designate megalithic monuments. They are not the original names, of course; they were given after all memory of the builders had been lost, apparently in the time of Celtic domination.

What is the meaning of "Stonehenge?" The first part, "stone," poses no problem. The second part, "henge," seems to have come from Old English *hon* (preterit *heng,* past participle *hongen*), meaning "to hang." The name may thus mean "hanging stones," an allusion either to the lintels resting on the uprights or to a gallows, for it is possible that the trilithons were used as gallows during a certain period, or that they were simply compared to gallows. Near Amesbury, on the road to Stonehenge, is a place called Gallows Hill. In a drawing reproduced in the French magazine *Historia,** the name "Stonehenge" appears inside an ornamental scroll, and beside it is written in French, "That is, hanging stones." Wace, an Anglo-Norman poet, wrote, "They are named Stanhenges in English, Hanging Stones in French."

In the fourteenth century a clumsy draftsman tried to make an isometric drawing of Stonehenge. Unfortunately, his simplified sketch depicts a kind of rectangular peristyle that would be hard to recognize as Stonehenge without the accompanying text. The author evidently intended to depict the Sarsen Circle, excluding the other stones. The trilithons are not shown at all, and we can deduce nothing about the state of the monument at the time when the drawing was made.

**Historia,* No. 166, Sept., 1960. The drawing in question dates from 1588. It appears in *A Particular Description of England* by William Smith. It is a copy of the 1574 drawing mentioned later.

The Latin text can be translated as follows: "Stonehenges, near Amesbury, England. In the year 483 the enchanter Merlin, solely by virtue of his art and not by force, brought the Dance of the Giants from Ireland to Stonehenges." The drawing and the text are in a manuscript in the library of Corpus Christi College at Cambridge. The text shows that three centuries after Geoffrey of Monmouth, Stonehenge was still the Dance of the Giants. Efforts were later made to revive that name, but without success.

Stonehenge and the Devil

It would have been surprising if the devil had not been associated with Stonehenge in one way or another. One story that makes that association must have been invented in the fifteenth or sixteenth century, although it did not appear in print till 1660. Here is a summary of it:

The prophet Merlin, wishing to build a lasting monument on Salisbury Plain, asked the devil for help in transporting the necessary stones, which were in Ireland, guarded by an old woman. The devil went to her dressed as a gentleman and offered to buy the stones from her in the following way: She would receive as much money as she could count during the time it took him to lift and move them. Thinking she was dealing with an ordinary mortal, the old woman eagerly accepted the bargain. The devil placed in front of her a purse filled with coins whose values were rather inconvenient for counting, such as four and a half pence, nine pence, and thirteen and a half pence, but she thought she would have time to add up a large sum while he tried to carry out his impossible task. Surely she would become richer than a princess.

But as soon as she had touched the first coin, the devil told her to stop. The stones were ready to be taken away. She looked around and was amazed to see that they were bound together like an enormous faggot. The devil picked them up on his shoulder and flew off toward Salisbury Plain with them. On the way, the rope holding the stones together began hurting him, and he shifted the load to his other shoulder, but one of the stones came loose and fell into the Avon, at Bulford, where it still remains.* The rest safely arrived at the chosen place, and the devil went to work.

It was midnight. Shortly before dawn, as he was about to put the last stone in place, satisfied with his work, he said aloud, "No one will ever know how these stones came here, or from where." A monk who had spent the night nearby replied, "You're certainly right about that," or something similar. Furious, the devil picked up the stone and threw it at the monk. The monk ran away, but the stone hit him on the heel. It still bears the mark, and that is why it is called the Heel Stone or the Friar's Heel.

Whatever the time when this tale was invented, it shows the influence of Geoffrey of Monmouth's story since it involves Merlin and places the origin of the stones in Ireland. But it is rather lacking in imagination and coherence. Merlin, who might be expected to help the devil or work under his guidance, remains in the background—unless the version of the tale that has come down to us is incomplete. One observation: In neither this story nor Geoffrey of Monmouth's is there any reference to the name of the sarsen stones, that is, the Saracen stones.

The legend of the devil is only a reflection of a feeling often aroused by the sight of Stonehenge. That monument, unique in the world, seems to have come there by magic, and the devil's words convey that impression: "No one will ever know how these stones came here, or from where."

According to John Aubrey—an author of whom I will speak in the next section, and who was probably the first to report the legend of the devil—the stone thrown at the monk was not the Heel Stone, but up-

*It is interesting to compare this story with the legend of Mont Saint-Michel in which the devil, obliged by the archangel to build the edifice, carries stones bound together on his shoulders and drops a few of them on the way.

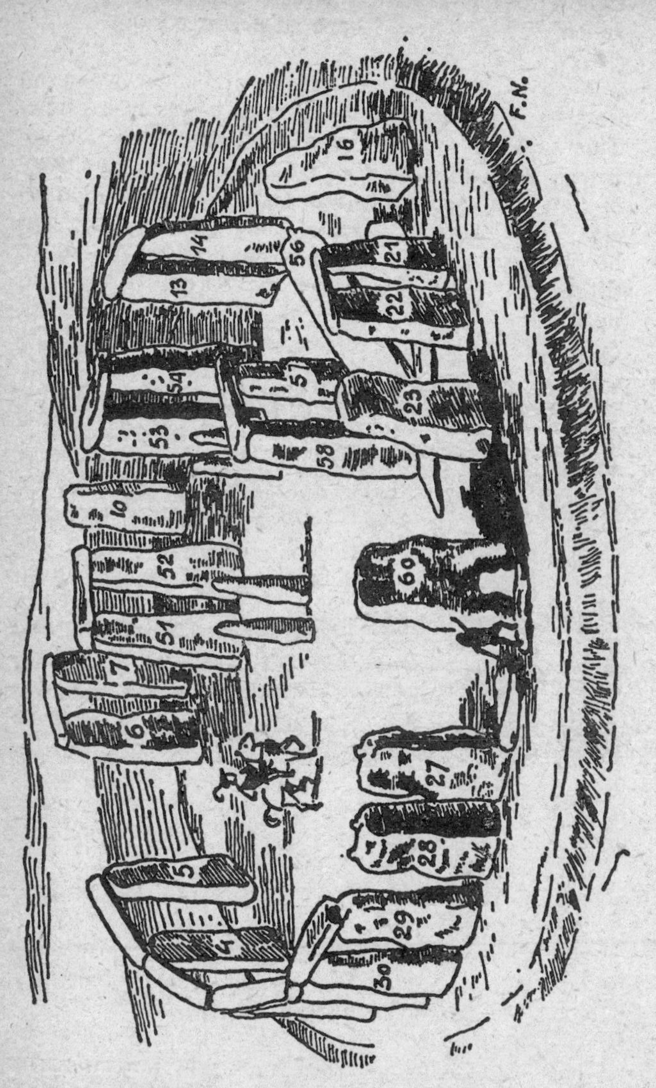

FIGURE 15—Dutch drawing dated 1574.

right 14 of the Sarsen Circle, now lying on the ground. In it is a cavity vaguely shaped like a large foot.

In 1574 another anonymous draftsman made an isometric drawing of Stonehenge as it was in his time. This drawing appears in a manuscript now in the British Museum, written in Dutch and titled, *Summary of Events in England, According to the Best Chronicles.* The draftsman made a commendable effort, but he also made two notable mistakes. Upright 60 of trilithon 59–60 is shown in the Sarsen Circle, and upright 56 of the Great Trilithon is shown leaning outward, whereas it was actually leaning inward. The drawing has one interesting detail, however: At the time when it was made, uprights 13 and 14 of the Sarsen Circle were still in place and joined by their lintel. If any proof were needed, this would show that some of the stones have been taken away from the site.

In the following year, 1575, another drawing was made, signed with the initials R. F. It appears in an edition of Camden's *Brittaniae Descriptio,* published in 1789. Obviously inspired by the preceding one, this drawing reproduces the two errors pointed out above. Furthermore, it shows two men digging up human bones, and on a hill in the background is a structure resembling a fortified castle. A caption says:

> This sheweth the order and manner of a most ancient monument in England, called Stohing, situate in the plain of Salisbury, being first brought out of Ireland by Uther Pendragon brother to Aurelius Ambrosius then king of the Britons through the help and counsel of Merlin, and there erected for a memory of certain noble Britons in the place slain by Hengist and his Saxons.

This second drawing calls for a few more remarks. Inside the circular earthwork we see two stones that do not appear in the drawing made the year before. Judging from their position in relation to the point from

FIGURE 16—Drawing made in 1575, signed R.F.

which the drawing was made (looking south), they may be the Heel Stone and the Slaughter Stone. If so, the latter was still standing in 1575. The men digging up bones seem to be outside the earthwork. They might be digging into a round barrow, or station 94. The practice of making excavations is rather old.

But something else appears in the picture. The draftsman seems to have deliberately tried to show an incoherent image. The order of the previous drawing is disrupted. This is a kind of caricature of Stonehenge. The stones appear to be writhing, as if they were in the grip of a fit of madness, and they make us feel the story of the devil coming on. Some of the lintels are cylindrical. The tenons of two uprights are exaggerated, as though they were meant to represent a woman's breasts. In the caption, the lintels are called "coronet stones" and the uprights "corpse stones."

The intention of caricaturing Stonehenge is even

FIGURE 17—Camden's drawing.

more obvious in a third drawing, not dated but reproduced in the fifth edition of Camden's *Britanniae Descriptio*, published in 1600. It was inspired by the previous one since we again see a castle in the background and men digging for bones. The castle has the appearance of a small town, however, and from its direction it might represent Amesbury, although that town cannot be seen from Stonehenge. Furthermore, the caption gives the same indications on the weight and size of the stones, and it also calls them "coronet stones" and "corpse stones."

But here the stones have a completely different appearance. They no longer seem to be writhing, but they are rough and jagged, as if they were meant to symbolize flames. Some of the uprights have profiles of human faces, as in those children's puzzles in which the problem is to find as many hidden people as possible. This is a Dantean Stonehenge. The artist has increased the incoherence, drawing lintels that lie at right angles to each other or form three sides of a rectangle. It is rather hard to identify the stones in that disorder, which gives us an even stronger impression that we are seeing the work of the devil or a madman. And Camden himself called Stonehenge "*insana substructio.*"

Royal Curiosity

But the influence of the devil did not affect certain less credulous and more cultivated minds. In 1613 the poet Michael Drayton called Stonehenge "the first wonder of the land" in his *Polyolbion,* a long description of England in verse.

At about that same time, someone decided to leave his name to posterity by carving it, or having it carved, on the inside of upright 53 of trilithon 53–54, at a man's height. The name is Johannes Ludovicus de Ferre, abbreviated to IOH : LVD : DEFERRE. The inscription is remarkably regular and was done by someone who knew how to use a chisel. The letter E has the shape of the Greek letter sigma, which has made some visitors believe that the inscription is in

Greek, perhaps one of those mentioned by Diodorus Siculus.

Some very different dates have been proposed for the construction of Stonehenge. The latest one seems to be the tenth century, put forward in 1663 by Walter Charleton in his book *Chorea Gigantum, Vulgarly Called Stone-Heng, Restored to the Danes*. The Danes took control of England in the late tenth and early eleventh centuries. According to Charleton, while their main army was in Wiltshire, they built or rebuilt Stonehenge to make it the place where their kings were elected and crowned.

The first great studies of Stonehenge were made in the seventeenth century, and the impetus may have come from the Duke of Buckingham. George Villiers, Duke of Buckingham, is well known as a character in *The Three Musketeers*. He was educated in France. He had a whimsical disposition and led a very active political life. How did he find time to take an interest in Stonehenge? In 1620 he was residing at Wilton with King Charles I, whose favorite he was. Wilton, about 4 miles from Salisbury, is not far from Stonehenge, and the duke probably saw the monument while he was horseback riding on Salisbury Plain. We do not know if he was looking for treasure, but he had excavations made.

Stonehenge was then part of a farm where a lady named Mary Trotman lived. She witnessed the excavations, and we know their results through her. The finds were not very impressive: deer antlers, ox horns, arrowheads, and a few fragments of rusty armor. For a long time the fall of the Great Trilithon was attributed to those excavations, but discovery of the drawings described in the preceding section made it possible to date its fall at a time earlier than the second half of the sixteenth century.

The Duke of Buckingham must have spoken of Stonehenge to King Charles I with enthusiasm, because the king also wanted to see that curious monument. In anticipation of the questions he might want to ask, he brought along his chief architect, Inigo Jones.

In 1621, the year of the royal visit to Stonehenge, Inigo Jones was 48 years old and a famous man. His teacher had been the brilliant Palladio. He introduced what was known as the Palladian style into England. His contemporaries went so far as to call him the Vitruvius of his time. When the king asked him for an explanation of Stonehenge, he answered, since he had to say something, without much conviction, "It is a Roman work in the ancient Tuscan style, dedicated to the god Coelus."

Stonehenge had made a deep impression on him. He took measurements, probably in haste, with the idea of theoretically reconstructing the original state of the monument. He also made drawings of what he saw. In them we feel the hand of a master, and we finally see the real Stonehenge. Unfortunately, his work on the subject was not published during his lifetime, and consequently he did not revise it as he might have before sending it to a printer. His son-in-law, John Webb, assembled all his notes and drawings and published them in 1655, four years after his death, under the title *Inigo Jones, Esquire, Architect General to the King. The Most Notable Antiquity of Great Britain, Vulgarly Called Stone-Heng, on Salisbury Plain, Restored by Inigo Jones, Esquire.*

The eminent architect had realized what was most amazing about the monument: the architectural knowledge that its construction presupposed. He was aware of Geoffrey of Monmouth's explanation, but he could not accept it; the ancient Britons seemed to him too ignorant to have built such a unique structure. Imbued with ancient classicism, he therefore concluded that it was the work of the Romans. His drawings of the monument in its original state have an exaggerated geometrical regularity that does indeed make one think of a Roman, Greek, or Egyptian temple. We can overlook the mistake he made in drawing six trilithons arranged in a hexagon. That may have been what he himself would have done if he had built Stonehenge.

FIGURE 18—Drawing by Inigo Jones, 1621.

His overall plan also has a distressing geometrical regularity. He placed three entrances in the ditch and bank, which was probably accurate, but he flanked each of them with four pillars. Later investigators racked their brains to decide whether those stones, or at least those at the opening of the Avenue, had really existed in his time. His book was nevertheless the first one devoted solely to Stonehenge, and it drew the attention of "antiquaries" to the mysterious monument.

One of the most remarkable of those "antiquaries" was John Aubrey. Born in 1626, he was about 40 years old when he first took an interest in Stonehenge. He had traveled a great deal and planned to write a long book entitled *Templa Druidum,* whose first volume would be devoted to British monuments.* That plan was to lead him all over England, and it was thus that he called attention to the great cromlech of Avebury. He naturally attributed it and Stonehenge to the Druids. He therefore seems to have been one of those responsible for that famous theory, although he confessed that it was only "a groping in darkness."

He gave us some more or less interesting details. For example, he said that in his time the stones of Stonehenge were thought to have special properties. This can be compared with the legend of Merlin. He also referred to the legend of the devil, but opinion was divided as to which stone was thrown at the monk. It was the Heel Stone according to some, the Slaughter Stone according to others; still others regarded upright 14 in the Sarsen Circle as the most likely. As for Aubrey, he believed that the legend was attached to a large stone "which lies on the west side." The question is not very important except in relation to the origin of the name of the Heel Stone.

It was Aubrey who, according to Mary Trotman, held the Duke of Buckingham responsible for the fall of the Great Trilithon. But the most interesting part of his work is a plan, a kind of freehand sketch, which he entitled, "Iconography of Stonehenge, as it exists in this year of 1666." In it, the outline of the monument is partially restored. There are thirty uprights in the Sarsen Circle and an equal number of stones in the Bluestone Circle. In the Bluestone Horseshoe and the trilithons, only those stones still standing are shown.

The most surprising feature of the sketch is that three stones are shown at the entrance of the monument, on the side of the Avenue, at exactly the same place where Inigo Jones showed four. Since the Heel Stone is also depicted, these were meant to be distinct stones, only one of which, the Slaughter Stone, still remains. If we compare this with the two stones indicated in the 1575 drawing, we might conclude that in

*To the best of my knowledge, this work was not published. It is said to exist only in manuscript in the Bodleian Library at Oxford.

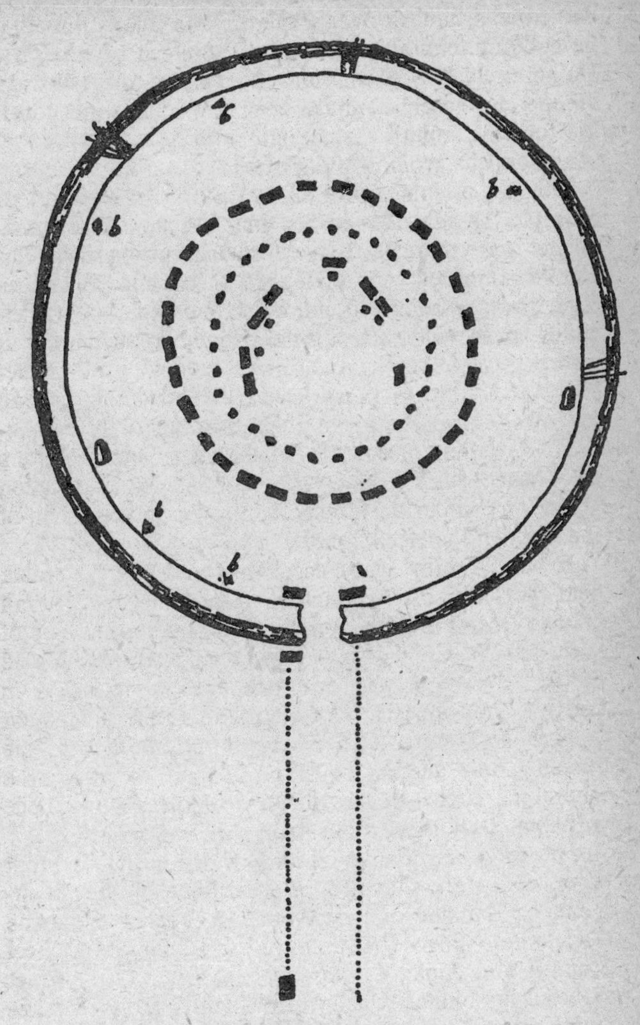

FIGURE 19—Sketch by John Aubrey, 1666.

the first half of the seventeenth century the Slaughter Stone and its companion were still standing.

In connection with those stones that are now missing but seem to have still existed in the seventeenth century, the memorialist John Evelyn wrote in his diary that he had counted ninety-five stones at Stonehenge, ten more than there are today. All this seems to show that the number of stones was greater in the seventeenth century than now. The indications given by Inigo Jones and John Aubrey may therefore not have been very inaccurate, although perhaps they made the mistake, as I have already suggested, of believing that stones that had been moved and were ready to be broken up and taken away were still in their original positions.

In the drawings I discussed in the preceding section, uprights 12, 13, and 14 of the Sarsen Circle seem to be standing in their original positions, the latter two with their lintel in place. But in the precise plans that were drawn later, only upright 14 is shown, either tilted or lying on the ground. So between 1580 and 1650 at least one sarsen upright disappeared completely. That may have been a period in which a particularly large number of stones were taken away from the monument, which would explain the surprising features of the drawings by Inigo Jones and John Aubrey. Uprights 13 and 14 are thought to have fallen in about 1594. Upright 14 was narrower at its base than at its top and must not have been very stable.

In his sketch, Aubrey indicated five small, unevenly spaced depressions just inside the ditch and bank. Two and a half centuries later, this detail led to discovery of the fifty-six holes that came to be known as the Aubrey Holes.

William Stukeley

William Stukeley is certainly one of the most engaging figures in the history of Stonehenge. Remarkably intelligent, he had studied medicine at Oxford, where he showed outstanding ability in the sciences. And, judging from the countless quotations with which his works are studded, his knowledge of the classical humanities was equally extraordinary. By dint of practicing comparative anatomy on all the dead dogs he could find, he became a famous surgeon. He was a close friend of Newton. Afflicted with gout, he prescribed long horseback rides for himself, and it was probably during those outings that he became interested in studying the old monuments he encountered. A portrait of him shows a likable face with big, intelligent eyes and slightly mocking lips.

Let us look through his book, a large folio volume entitled *Stonehenge, a Temple Restored to the British Druids, by William Stukeley, M.D., Rector of All Saints in Stamford*. The epigraph is *"Deus est qui non mutatur in oevo,"* and farther down we learn that the work was printed in London in 1740. It is actually composed of two parts, one devoted to Stonehenge, the other to Avebury, at least in the edition I have seen.

The title leaves no room for doubt: Stonehenge is attributed to the Druids. The book is full of that idea. The monument, in fact, is said to have been the cathedral of the "Archdruids." To give some idea of the general tone of the book, here is the title of Chapter XII:

> A conjecture about the time of the founding of Stonehenge. —An uniforme variation in setting these works, not to be accounted for, but by supposing the Druids us'd a magnetical compass. —Their leader, the Tyrian Hercules, was possess'd of a compass-box. —The oracle of Jupiter Ammon had a compass-box. —The golden fleece at Colchis was a compass-box. —Both these temples were founded by Apher, Aphricus, or Phryxus; the same person seems to have given name to Britain. —The Druids set their temple and other works by it. —The history of the variation of the magnetic needle. —A conjecture of the time of building Stonehenge from thence.

Then comes a text stuffed with quotations from ancient authors, well designed to convince Stukeley's contemporaries.

He vehemently attacks John Webb, Inigo Jones's son-in-law. Scandalized by Jones's theoretical reconstruction, he appeals to trigonometry and Lord Pembroke's measurements to demonstrate that it is a gross error. He finds that Stonehenge was built with a cubit of 20.8 inches, divided into six palms. This is the cubit of the Druids, Hebrews, Egyptians, and Phoenicians. Carried away by his enthusiasm, he takes it back to Noah or Adam. To him, the gigantic cromlech of Avebury and its Kennet Avenue represent the head and body of a serpent. And the whole structure, under the name of Dracontia, was a temple dedicated to worship of the serpent. We may smile, but let us not laugh aloud. He indignantly compares the work of the local peasants, who broke up the stones of the cromlech, to the autos-da-fé of the Spanish Inquisition.

His numerous drawings reveal a keen sense of observation and undoubtedly correspond to reality, but like Inigo Jones, he shows stones whose geometrical regularity is much too perfect. His plan abounds in triangles, circles, and ellipses. His many views of Stonehenge and the environs show considerable artistic talent. There are always a few people in them: ladies or gentlemen in costumes of the time, Stukeley himself on horseback, or a Druid meditating amid the ruins.

Stukeley idealized Stonehenge. It had literally captivated him. He wrote of being plunged in an "ecstatic revery" at the sight of it. He had a miniature Stonehenge built in his garden, where he had a plum tree covered with mistletoe. His enthusiasm for the Druids increased with age. His profession was medicine, but he decided to be ordained as a minister, convinced that his mission in this world was to reconcile Christianity with the ancient religion of the Celts. He died in 1765. Shortly before his death he had to wear spectacles for his frequent reading, and when, at the age of 76, he preached a sermon with his spectacles perched on his nose, he chose as his text: "For now we see through a glass, darkly."

But let us leave that rather eccentric Stukeley and become acquainted with the other one, the real one, one of the best observers who ever studied Stonehenge, if not the best.

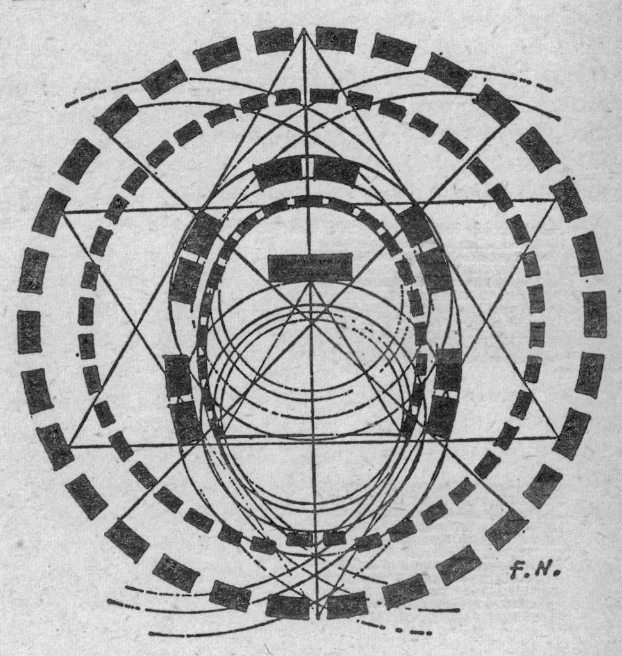

FIGURE 20—How Stukeley made his theoretical reconstruction of Stonehenge.

He was the first to determine the exact number and positions of the stones. A reconstructed plan drawn in 1950 differed very little from his. His sense of observation was especially surprising with regard to the number of bluestones. He placed forty in the circle and nineteen in the horseshoe; these figures were later altered, but they have come to be accepted in our time. He saw that stones 49 and 31 of the circle were tangent to it at their outer rather than their inner surfaces. This shows his skill in taking measurements.

He was probably the first to notice one fact, which later made a stir: the general orientation of the structure toward sunrise at the summer solstice. He also recognized the relationship between the Four Stations and the circle, and he wrote with regard to the mounds, "The two cavities in the circuit of our area very probably were the places where two great stone vases were set." It was not until Colonel Hawley's excavations in 1920 that the accuracy of that observation was confirmed.

He recognized the nature of the sarsens and discovered the Avenue and the Cursus in the environs. His measurements of those two works were later recognized as accurate to within a few inches. The same is true of the orientation of the Cursus. He blamed magnetic variation for its 7-degree departure from the east-west line. (Here again, let us content ourselves with smiling.) Aided by Lord Pembroke, he excavated barrows, found sarsen and bluestone fragments, and related them to Stonehenge. He reported that "at present" the Slaughter Stone was lying on the ground, which shows that he may not have been wholly convinced that it had once been used as a sacrificial stone. Nothing escaped him. He noted all details; for example, the stone of station 91, which was then tilted and is now on the ground.

Personally, I cannot dissociate Stonehenge from Stukeley. He oriented his research toward rational and purely scientific aims. His application of trigonometry to the monument served, if not to take measurements, at least to verify them. Although it is unreliable, his system of dating the monument by means of magnetic variation was a remarkable anticipation of methods that were to be used later. He tried to determine the unit of measurement used by the builders of Stonehenge and was thus the precursor of Petrie and others in the study of a subject capable of giving important information on the origin of Stonehenge.

Yet he has been violently taken to task by certain archaeologists in modern times. He is regarded as one of those responsible for the Druidic and Celtic mania that was rampant among antiquaries in the eighteenth and nineteenth centuries. His ideas passed over to the continent, where the megalithic monuments were also attributed to the Celts. In France, dolmens were thought to have been sacrificial tables. For some archaeologists, all of Stukeley's merits are wiped away by his attribution of Stonehenge to the Druids.

Let us put ourselves in Stukeley's place for a moment. Which of us would not have thought as he did to some extent? He started from scratch, with nothing at his disposal but ancient authors and the monument itself. He did not have behind him the three or four generations of researchers and excavators who have gradually revealed the existence of populations earlier than the Celts. If some people still believe that Stonehenge was built by the Druids and that sacrifices were performed on the Slaughter Stone and the slabs of dolmens, does it really matter? In our time, it is said, the ashes of members of neo-Druidic sects are secretly buried under the turf of Stonehenge. It would not be hard to find equally bizarre practices among the other religious sects that abound in the modern world.

As for Stukeley, in spite of his errors and exaggerations, he remains the great precursor. If he had lived in our time, the secret of Stonehenge might now have been discovered.

Choir Gaur

This expression, strange at first sight, is the main title of two works published in the eighteenth century, twenty-four years apart. It is a Celticized form, derived from *Cor Gawr,* of the *Chorea Gigantum* of Charleton, who attributed Stonehenge to the Danes.

The first *Choir Gaur* is by John Wood, the great architect of Bath, one of whose works was the famous Royal Crescent. The book was published in 1747. In it, Wood writes that the ancient Britons called Stonehenge by the name of *Choir Gaur,* which was Latinized to *Chorea Gigantum* by monks and finally became "Dance of the Giants."

In about 1740 a man built a hut in the midst of the ruins, near stones 59 and 60. A native of Amesbury, he was called Gaffer Hunt. His dwelling seems to have been nothing but a smoky den. He had abandoned his trade as a carpenter to serve as a guide to Stonehenge visitors, which illustrates how people have always been interested in the monument. Stukeley must have known Gaffer Hunt. He was a "venerable man" and very loquacious. He knew all the stories and legends about Stonehenge and told them to anyone who would listen. Perhaps he invented some of them himself. In any case, it was he who told the story of the devil to John Wood, who was the first to transmit it to us since John Aubrey's book was never published.

For Wood, Stonehenge was a Druidic temple consecrated to the moon. He counted twenty-nine stones in the Bluestone Circle, rather, twenty-nine bluestone trilithons, but he deducted one to make their number correspond to the number of days in a lunar month. The two different kinds of stone were symbols of good and evil. The monument unquestionably showed the influence of Persian Magi and the Zoroastrian reform.

But the most interesting feature of Wood's book is a precise plan of the ruins as they existed in his time. He described the method he used in drawing up the plan, something his successors did not do. He first drew a hexagon with fairly equal sides, inscribed in the Sarsen Circle. He then drew several diagonals and, in relation to all those lines, took the ordinates of the vertices of the angles of the standing and lying stones. In the drawing, stone 22 of the Sarsen Circle and the uprights of trilithon 57–58, stones that later fell, are shown in their original positions. Stone 14 of the Sarsen Circle is shown still standing but leaning toward bluestone 38. Plans published after Wood's time show that stone lying in its present position.

All through the eighteenth century, Stukeley's opinion was not contested: Stonehenge was a Druidic temple. Cooke, Borlase, and many others agreed. Benjamin Martin revived a hypothesis that had been stated by

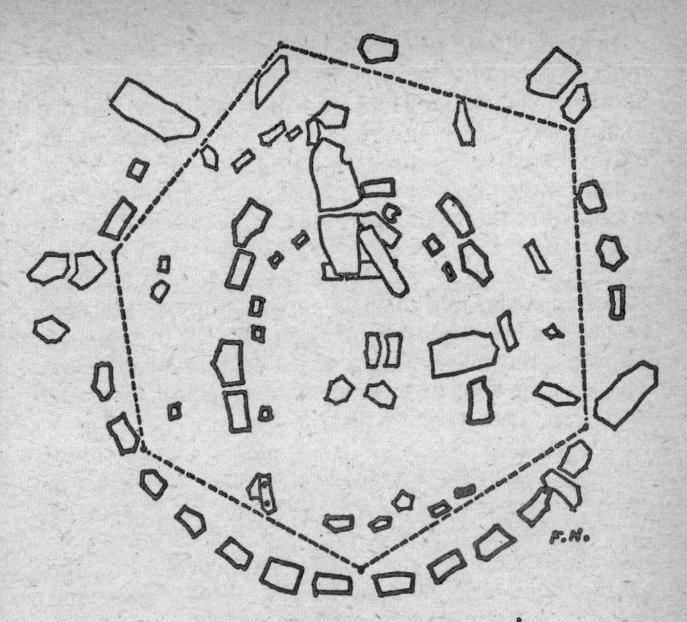

FIGURE 21—John Wood's plan, 1747.
(Dotted lines: the basic polygon he used in drawing his plan.)

several authors in Inigo Jones's time: that the stones of the monument were artificial, made of a kind of concrete. This idea came from the fact that there were no quarries in the vicinity from which the great sarsen blocks could have been taken. Even among the greywethers of the Marlborough Downs there were no stones of that size. The origin of the stones of Stonehenge continued to puzzle investigators.

The second *Choir Gaur* appeared in 1771, written by John Smith. Its complete title is *Choir Gaur; The Grand Orrery of the Ancient Druids, Commonly Called Stonehenge,* and its epigraph is *"Felix qui potuit rerum cognoscere causas."* ("Fortunate is he who can know the inner meaning of things.")

Smith divided the ditch and bank into twelve parts, corresponding to the signs of the zodiac. The five sarsen trilithons and two bluestone trilithons were symbols of the seven planets. The oval they described was none other than the *ovum mundi* of the ancients. There

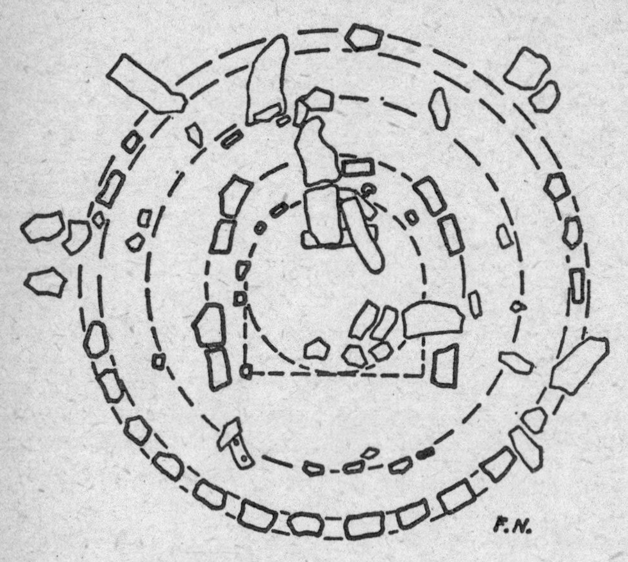

FIGURE 22—John Smith's plan.

were thirty uprights in the Sarsen Circle; if that number were multiplied by twelve, the result would be the number of days in the original solar year. And so on.

But in the midst of all that, Smith points out an important fact that Stukeley had glimpsed but not stated explicitly: on June 21, the day of the summer solstice, the sun, seen from the center of the monument, rises over the Heel Stone. The idea that astronomy might have something to say on the matter was beginning to make itself felt.

It is interesting to compare Smith's and Wood's plans of Stonehenge as it existed in their time. There are few differences between them, which testifies in favor of their accuracy. Smith also indicates the positions of stones 57, 58, and 22. In his theoretical reconstruction he places thirty bluestones in the circle and eleven in the horseshoe. He seems to have been the first to speak of two symmetrical bluestone trilithons. He shows them in his plan.

One opinion worth noting is that of Waltire, for whom Stonehenge was a vast theodolite intended for observation of the heavenly bodies. He believed it had a meridian line about 12 miles long at the time of its construction, and that this line formed an angle of 47 degrees with the north-south direction. As we can see, all sorts of ideas about Stonehenge have been stated, even from the standpoint of astronomy, and there are undoubtedly more to come.

On January 3, 1797, trilithon 57–58 collapsed under the following circumstances. During the preceding autumn some Gypsies had come to Stonehenge; rather than set up their dwellings at ground level, they dug a hole at the foot of the trilithon so that they could have a deeper shelter. At the beginning of winter they left, and the hole remained, constantly being filled with water and snow. On January 1, 1797, as the result of a heavy snowstorm, the trilithon began tilting. In the next two days it tilted more and more rapidly until finally it fell toward the west. Fortunately, both uprights and the lintel remained intact since there were no stones under them to make them break.

Sir Richard Colt Hoare

In the history of Stonehenge, the nineteenth century appears as a long transition period. The Druidic origin made fashionable by Stukeley was still accepted, along with other opinions that differed rather widely. That diversity can be explained by the unusual nature of the monument, but Stonehenge was nearly always regarded as representing the astronomical knowledge of its builders.*

*This tendency to regard Stonehenge as a vast astronomical observatory was again manifested in 1964, in a rather unexpected way. (See Appendix 3.)

In 1800, in his *Indian Antiquities,* Thomas Maurice gave six main reasons for assigning an astronomical purpose to the monument, beginning with its circular shape, which was appropriate for sun worship. Like John Smith, he believed that the oval of the "adytum" represented the world egg. The direction of the main entrance was also a weighty argument. That there were sixty stones in the Sarsen Circle, counting uprights and lintels, unquestionably showed a connection with the sexagesimal cycle of Asian astronomy, and the nineteen stones in the horseshoe represented a Metonic cycle. The open construction showed that the monument was built in the same spirit as the temples of the ancient Persians, who considered it impious to enclose the divinity in a temple. Finally, the ox heads and horns found in the enclosure were related to the bloodiest rites of solar superstition. (This again shows that people were in the habit of making excavations inside the monument.)

To John Britton, Stonehenge was clearly the work of the Romanized Britons, and to Reverend Edward Davies it was equally clear that the monument was one of the finest examples of Druidic superstition. Little by little, however, more accurate or plausible ideas were beginning to appear. As early as 1793, in a book titled *Nenia Britannica,* James Douglas wrote that Stonehenge had been built long before the time of the Druids, but that it had perhaps been used until the time of the Anglo-Saxons. Moreover, in the nineteenth century the new science of prehistory arose, and as its various disciplines were developed, they were applied to the study of Stonehenge. That period was thus a kind of preparation for the great scientific research of the following century.

The first half of the nineteenth century was dominated by the work of Sir Richard Colt Hoare. A tireless researcher, he excavated no less than 465 grave mounds on Salisbury Plain, aided by his faithful William Cunnington, in only a dozen years. All the objects found were carefully assembled; most of them are now in the Devizes Museum. In 1812 Colt Hoare published a two-volume work, *The Ancient History of Wilt-*

shire. Each volume has a format of 16 by 22 inches and weighs a goodly number of pounds. Five-inch margins reduce the text to more normal proportions, but a lectern is helpful in reading it. It is a beautiful book, containing many illustrations of the finest and most characteristic objects found in barrows. These objects—tools, ornaments, utensils, weapons—later made it possible to identify the Wessex Culture.

As far as Stonehenge was concerned, Colt Hoare contributed almost nothing original. He did not try to restore the monument. He attributed it to the Britons and believed they used it as a meeting place for civil or religious assemblies. He agreed with one of Stukeley's contentions: The sarsen and bluestone fragments found in the barrows showed that Stonehenge must have been built before or at the same time as the barrows.

He excavated stations 92 and 94; he discovered nothing in 92, but in 94 he found cremated remains, which caused it to be regarded as a grave mound for a long time. He gave the length of the Avenue as 1,781 feet, and at the end of that distance he traced two branches, one of them going to the Cursus. He believed the Cursus might have been used as a course for chariot races, an idea previously stated by Stukeley.

Still working with Cunnington, he studied the Slaughter Stone. Their excavations showed that it once stood on the end facing the Heel Stone and must have been sunk 3 feet into the ground. Before closing their excavations in that place, Cunnington left a bottle of port wine under the Slaughter Stone, presumably for the benefit of future archaeologists. It might be interesting to re-examine all the other places explored by Colt Hoare and his companion.

In the final analysis, Colt Hoare was a skeptic who asked himself no questions. When his friend suggested to him that the two kinds of stone might correspond to two distinct phases, he merely answered, *"Se non è vero, è bene trovato."* He was primarily a collector of ancient objects, and his greatest pleasure was to find something rare or unique in a grave. His conclusions never went beyond what was necessary to justify his overwhelming labor.

After Colt Hoare, Druidism and astronomical explanations were still in fashion. Like Thomas Maurice, Geoffrey Higgins, in his book *The Celtic Druids* (1829), stated that the sixty stones of the Outer Circle were related to the most famous cycles. As for the Bluestone Horseshoe, it represented the Metonic cycle of nineteen years. On the basis of astronomical considerations, Higgins concluded that Stonehenge had been built four thousand years before Christ. "A date," he added, "which will astonish most persons who have not been accustomed to examine subjects of this kind."

In *The Druidical Temples of the County of Wilts,* Reverend Edward Duke wrote that Stonehenge was one of seven planetariums in Wiltshire and represented Saturn. Browne, of Amesbury, was convinced that the stones had been eroded by water and that the monument therefore went back to a time before the Deluge. For Christian Maclagan, there was no doubt that the structure had been built for military defense.

In *Researches into the Lost Histories of America,* W. S. Blagkett wrote, "The Apalachian Indians, with their priests and medicine men, must have been the builders of Stonehenge. That great and marvellous erection, therefore, attests the truthfulness of Plato when he brings into Western Europe a great conquering people from beyond the Pillars of Hercules." And so Stonehenge lacks nothing, not even a relation, direct or indirect, to Atlantis.

Equally startling ideas can be found in literature. Here is an example:

> On Salisbury Plain stand the ruins of the weird Circle of Revolution, Cor y Coeth in Welsh, the Circle of Dominion, the holy anointed stones of Ambresbiri (*ambree,* anointed; *biri,* Hebrew for holy ones), at once a sanctuary and a sundial (3000 years ago the only clock in Britain), regulated by the sun and moon for days and years. But

the beautiful old British names since the sixth century have been blotted out by the terrible title Stonehenge, or stone gallows—Stanhangen in Anglo-Saxon.

And Charles Dickens, in his *Child's History of England,* said that Stonehenge was a temple consecrated to the strange and terrible religion of the Druids.

In about 1829 a mason passing through Stonehenge carved his initials on the lintel of the Great Trilithon and enclosed them in a curve resembling a question mark. There is nothing significant about this in itself; I am pointing it out because the whole carving was once thought to be a prehistoric date. The curve was seen as a sickle, attributed to the Druids, of course.

William Matthew Flinders Petrie

In 1872 James Fergusson published his book on megalithic monuments, *Rude Stone Monuments.* Stonehenge occupied an important place in it because Fergusson assigned a very late date to dolmens and menhirs, and with Geoffrey of Monmouth's story, Stonehenge was grist for his mill. He concluded that it was a cenotaph erected in honor of the noble Britons murdered by Hengist. His attempted reconstruction is highly debatable with regard to the bluestone structure.

At about the same time, William Long stated that the history of the monument might be determined from the contents of the barrows in the environs. The results obtained from excavations within Stonehenge itself, he felt, would be insignificant compared with the risk to the structure, as was shown by the fall of the Great Trilithon. The justification of such excavations would be to demonstrate that Stonehenge was not built as a burial place, but, he said, "even the discovery of human remains within the circles would no more prove that Stonehenge was constructed to be a burial place than the finding of bishops' and other people's bodies in cathedrals."

With Nevil Story Maskeline an important period begins. His book *Stonehenge; the Petrology of Its Stones*, published in 1877, inaugurated scientific studies to determine the origin and geological nature of the sarsens and bluestones. I will return to this subject later; its unexpected consequences make it particularly interesting.

While the first half of the nineteenth century is dominated by Colt Hoare's excavations of barrows, the second half is dominated by Petrie's studies. William Matthew Flinders Petrie, born in London in 1853, was primarily a great Egyptologist, but he also took an interest in Stonehenge. In the course of work carried out in 1877, he took extremely precise measurements of the monument, using special instruments, and drew an exact plan of the ruins at ground level. This plan was published on a scale of 1 to 200 in a small book entitled *Stonehenge—Plan, Description and Theories* (London, 1880).

Petrie's plan has been used by nearly all authors who have written on Stonehenge since his time. It would be hard to carry precision much further since his measurements were accurate to within a quarter of an inch. Because of its scale, the plan is not easy to use for studying details, but anyone who wants to draw a plan of his own can use Petrie's to avoid making any significant mistakes. Petrie also left us some extraordinarily accurate measurements of heights.

He was probably the first to verify that lines joining stations 91–93 and 92–94 intersect at the center of the monument and form 45-degree angles. This had been noticed by Reverend Duke in 1846 but not precisely verified. Petrie apparently ignored the Avenue in drawing his Axis—as he may have been right to do—and he made it pass through the center of the monument. On the basis of astronomical considerations he dated the monument, or at least the sarsen structure, at the year 730, with a margin of error of plus or minus two hundred years. He considered the bluestones to be more recent. He seemed to accept Geoffrey of Monmouth's story, at least its historical part.

Petrie also wrote *Inductive Metrology,* in which he showed how one could determine the units of measurement used in the construction of ancient monuments, and of course he applied his methods to Stonehenge. He found that a single unit had apparently not been used for all parts of the monument. For example, a cubit of 22.5 inches, of Phoenician origin, seemed to have been used for laying out the ditch and bank, and a Roman foot equal to 11.7 inches for the sarsen structure. He concluded that the monument had been built in several stages, in this order: ditch and bank, Avenue, sarsen structure (circle, trilithons, stations, Slaughter Stone, Heel Stone), bluestone structure. Finally, to the best of my knowledge, it was Petrie who invented the system of numbering the stones that has since been adopted unanimously.

With regard to Petrie's Phoenician cubit, I will point out that in his time several archaeologists believed that the bold sailors of Tyre and Sidon had something to do with the construction of Stonehenge. Dr. Phéné found similar monuments at Saint-Nazaire and Ouessant and in the Mediterranean basin, and he concluded that they were of Phoenician origin because of the tin route. The similar monuments are the trilithons of Tripolitania and elsewhere, to which I referred earlier.

Reverend Lukis, of the Antiquaries Society in London, exemplified a more cautious and skeptical tendency. He felt that the Heel Stone had no connection with the monument because it was the only sarsen stone that showed no trace of tooling.

Various works, such as those of E. T. Stevens, W. Cunnington, T. A. Wise, John Rhys, and A. T. Evans, were published in the late nineteenth century, some more important than others. I will make special mention of *Stonehenge and Its Earthworks* (London, 1895) by Edgar Barclay. It is remarkably illustrated with reproductions of paintings and the drawings of Inigo Jones and Stukeley. Barclay related Stonehenge to old British traditions and concluded that it was of Roman-Celtic origin. Aside from that, he made many well-founded remarks. He was the first, as far as I know, to point out one curious detail: If the Slaughter Stone were standing, it would hide half of the Heel Stone, seen from the center of the monument. No one has since discussed that point, again as far as I know.

Barclay had the merit of not "juggling away" the anomaly presented by stone 11 or placing the point for observing the sun behind the central bluestone of the horseshoe. According to him, stone 11 marked the entrance of the temple, which is not at all unreasonable. He situated the observation point far behind stone 67, on the surrounding bank, so that the observer could look over it. This is certainly no more implausible than assuming that stone 67 was transparent, or that it was laid flat on the ground during observations and then erected again afterward.

By the end of the nineteenth century there was thus a more rational view of Stonehenge, and the nonlocal origin of its stones, particularly the bluestones, had been perceived. With Sir John Lubbock (*Prehistoric Times*) and C. I. Elton, Stonehenge came to be dated from the Bronze Age. The idea of a Druidic origin was completely abandoned by scientists and relegated to a few sects with mystical leanings.

On December 31, 1900, as the result of a violent windstorm, upright 22 of the Sarsen Circle fell to the ground, taking a lintel down with it. Superstitious minds saw this as a portent of Queen Victoria's death, which occurred three weeks later. The fall of upright 22 was one of the main causes of the measures that were taken to preserve the monument. Concern had been expressed long before, especially with regard to the deplorable practice of certain local innkeepers who supplied their guests with hammers so that they could break off chips of stone to keep as souvenirs.* I will not describe the maneuvers and court decisions that finally led to Stonehenge being classified as a historical monument and government property. By then, unfortunately, some important elements had been lost forever.

*It is the Altar Stone that seems to have suffered most from this.

I will end this section with a bibliographical curiosity to which I have already alluded. In 1902, in volume XXXII of the *Wiltshire Archaeological Magazine,* W. J. Harrisson published a 170-page article entitled "Bibliography of Stonehenge and Avebury." It listed about eight hundred books and articles, and three-quarters of them concerned Stonehenge.

The Work of Sir Joseph Norman Lockyer

The idea was in the air. That the monument is generally oriented toward sunrise at the summer solstice (as had been noted long before) called for an examination by astronomical specialists, who felt that precise measurements would make it possible to date the structure. Those measurements were relatively simple since they consisted only in determining two angles with a common side: the local meridian. For one angle, the second side is the axis of the monument; for the other, the present point of sunrise. The difference between them is caused by the phenomenon of precession, which is now well known and enables us to calculate the time taken to produce the difference.

This requires extremely accurate measurements, but the way had been paved by the British Ordnance Survey Department in surveys of the region made in about 1820 and 1880. I have already spoken of the Ordnance Survey axis and pointed out that the surveyors noticed this fact: If the axis of the Avenue is extended in both directions, it passes through two ancient earthworks on either side of the monument, Sidbury Hill and Grovely Castle. It also passes through the middle of the space between stones 1 and 30 of the Sarsen Circle. The azimuth of that line (that is, the angle it forms with the meridian) given by the Ordnance Survey is 49°34′18″. The latitude of Stonehenge, also as calculated by the Ordnance Survey, is 51°10′42″. Azimuth and latitude are basic elements in dating the monument by the astronomical method.

The azimuth of a heavenly body at the point of its

appearance above the horizon is a function of two factors: the latitude of the place and declination. In the case of the sun, the latter depends on the date. The sun's declination is an angle that changes every day, going from minus 23°27′ at the winter solstice to plus 23°27′ at the summer solstice, passing through a value of zero at the equinoxes. In France, its value is given for each day of the year in the *Annuaire du Bureau des Longitudes*. This angle of 23°27′ is equal to the inclination of the axis of the earth's rotation to the plane of its orbit, or plane of the ecliptic. The three elements, azimuth (at rising or setting), declination, and latitude, are related to each other by a formula of spherical trigonometry:

$$\sin \text{Declination} = \cos \text{Azimuth} \times \cos \text{Latitude}$$

With the data of the Ordnance Survey, we have:

$$\sin \text{Declination} = \cos 49°34' \times \cos 51°11'$$

This gives an angle of about 23°59′, 32 minutes greater than the 23°27′ of the present declination. Therefore, if at the time when Stonehenge was built its axis was aligned with sunrise at the summer solstice, the declination was 32 minutes greater than it is today. Since declination diminishes by about 47.6 seconds per century, it would have taken about forty centuries to produce a difference of 32 minutes.

That, in simplified form, is the problem of dating Stonehenge by the astronomical method. An attempt to solve it was made in 1901 by Sir Joseph Norman Lockyer, Astronomer Royal and director of the Solar Physics Laboratory in South Kensington.

After several trials he adopted the Ordnance Survey azimuth of 49°34′18″ for his calculations. To observe the sun, he chose the observation point behind stone 56 of the Great Trilithon and waited till the edge of the solar disk was two minutes of angle above the horizon, an angle equal to a sixteenth of the sun's diameter. This gave him a sufficient portion of the disk to perform the bisection and measure the angle. He obtained an azimuth of 50°26′30″, corresponding to a declination of 23°27′6″. He took other factors into account, notably the height of the horizon, equal to 35′30″. The formula given above is valid only for a horizon at the observer's height. Furthermore it gives the azimuth of the center of the sun at the time of its appearance on the horizon, that is, when half of the solar disk has emerged. Lockyer believed that the builders had oriented their axis toward the point on the horizon at which the sun first appeared.

He finally obtained a declination of 23°54′30″, differing appreciably from the one obtained above by a simple application of the formula. Using Stockwell's tables for calculating the obliquity of the ecliptic, published in 1873, he proposed the date of 1680 B.C.,

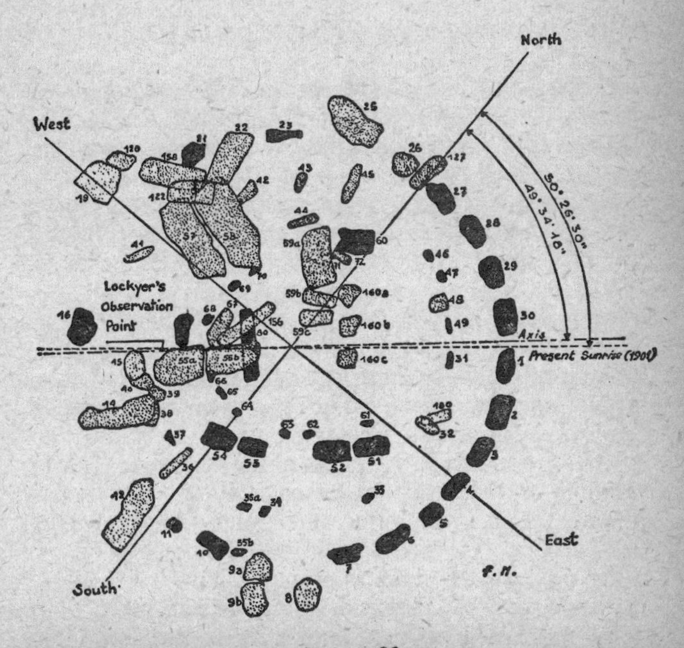

FIGURE 23

with a margin of plus or minus two hundred years to allow for possible errors of observation. Later, when the progressive decrease of the obliquity of the ecliptic was calculated more precisely, that date was changed to 1840 B.C., with the same margin of error. Lockyer first published the results of his work in *An Attempt to Ascertain the Date of the Original Construction of Stonehenge from its Orientation.* Later, in 1906, when he had applied his method to other ancient monuments, he published *Stonehenge and Other British Stone Monuments Astronomically Considered.*

Lockyer's work caused a sensation at the time, especially since an almost identical date had recently been arrived at by other methods. It had been decided to lift upright 56 of the Great Trilithon, which old drawings show as strongly tilted. The operation was carried out between April 18 and September 25, 1901, by an engineer and an architect under the guidance of Professor William Gowland. Excavations were made around the stone. Besides some objects of no great importance—Roman coins, a penny bearing the head of George III, bluestone and sarsen chips, flint axes—they revealed a sarsen fragment with a small greenish spot on it. Analysis showed that it was a trace of carbonate of copper.

Gowland was puzzled by this find. The spot of copper corresponded to no fragment of a tool or an instrument. It could only be from an ornament. The conclusion was that copper was known at the time when Stonehenge was built, which tallied with the date deduced by Lockyer. Such a correlation between the results of two totally different methods seemed extraordinary. But that union between astronomy and archaeology was to be short-lived.

Criticisms of Lockyer's work were not always very apt. That astronomer was regarded as an intruder in the realm of archaeology. Many criticisms came from the fact that the orientation of certain ancient monuments toward significant positions of the sun was not an idea favored by some prehistorians, who were more concerned with excavating than with studying remains on the surface. Other criticisms came from great ignorance of even the most elementary notions of cosmography. It is hard for some people to imagine why anyone should have built such large monuments to indicate something that can be looked up in an almanac.

But I will mention one curious criticism. In 1912, John Abercromby thought he had found the secret of Stonehenge on the basis of the principle that in any temple, no matter what its period or religion, one never turns toward the entrance, after one has come through it, to face the point where worship is celebrated. Therefore, the purpose of Stonehenge was not to celebrate the rising of the sun at the summer solstice, rather its setting at the winter solstice. And Sir Arthur Evans, the explorer of the Minoan temples, maintained that the monument had a sepulchral form related to the lower world. It was a temple in which the Great Trilithon represented the gate of the world of shadows. Through the uprights, the sun was observed at the time when, having reached the end of its course, it seemed to sink into the underworld.

With a monument like Stonehenge, we must be resigned to expecting anything.

It was possible to make more serious objections to Lockyer's work, however. First of all, his choice of the observation point behind the Great Trilithon. As I have said earlier, stone 67 apparently stood between that point and the point at which the sun rose above the horizon. Stone 67, now lying on the ground, was once on the axis of the monument. Otherwise there would have been no axis of symmetry, at least as far as the horseshoe was concerned. The stone would have had to be offset to permit observation through the space between the uprights of the Great Trilithon.

Furthermore, it is a mistake to believe that the axis of the Avenue is a prolongation of the axis of the monument, which, as I have pointed out, was laid out without regard to the center of the structure or the impressive arrangement of the trilithons. Strictly speaking, it is alien to the monument; it intersects the Sarsen Circle at the center of the space between stones 1 and 30, and that is all. It passes five or six inches away from the center, and its deviation has led to attributing exaggerated lengths to intervals 55–56 and 15–16.

Finally, Lockyer assumed that the point of aim on the horizon was the point at which the upper edge of the sun emerged. I will discuss that question later. But his assumption might have seemed dubious to him since in spite of his precise instruments he had to wait till the sun had partially risen above the horizon before he could take his measurements.

Lockyer's work was based on the part of the monument least suited to precise measurements: the earthworks. And if it is true that the Avenue was oriented toward sunrise at the summer solstice, his results led to assigning an approximate date to the Avenue and not to the monument itself.

Colonel Hawley's Excavations

In the history of Stonehenge, the first two decades of the twentieth century were not a very fruitful time. They were marked mainly by controversies between Lockyer and his critics. There was also the publication of a little guidebook, *Stonehenge Today and Yesterday*, by Frank Stevens, curator of the Salisbury Museum. It served as a guide for tens of thousands of visitors for twenty years, until Newall's book was published.

Toward the end of World War I a military airport was built near Amesbury. The military authorities then asked, with perfect seriousness, that Stonehenge be destroyed because its stones might be a danger to low-flying aircraft. It is easy to imagine the consternation and rage that must have seized British archaeologists when they learned of that request.

But the presence of airfields near Stonehenge was not without advantages. In the summer of 1921, aerial photographs of the region were taken by a squadron of the Royal Air Force, and examination of them revealed surprising details. In some places the grass or grain growing in fields was darker than elsewhere, and this was all the more surprising because the dark parts, sharply delimited, often appeared in the shape of a crown. The explanation was soon found.

Salisbury Plain, as I have said, is formed by a thin layer of soil over a layer of compact chalk. Wherever digging has gone down into the underlying layer, for one reason or another, roots can sink more deeply into the fragmented chalk mixed with earth. Plants grow higher at such places, and although this is hard to see from the surface, it is clearly visible from the air. It was in this way that Woodhenge was discovered, as well as many round barrows and the branches of the Avenue reported by Stukeley. It may have been the first time when aviation helped archaeology. Aerial photographs of the monument had already been taken before World War I.

In September 1923, Crawford and Passmore began searching for the places revealed by the aerial photographs. These pictures were their only guide since all vestiges had vanished from the surface. The outline of the Avenue was recognized to be as Stukeley had reported it, to within a foot. It was seen that after running in a straight line for more than 2,000 feet, the Avenue turned east, passed between two groups of barrows (the "new and old barrows of the king," to use the imaginative Stukeley's expression), and nearly reached the Avon, near Amesbury, after having described a large curve. One curious detail: Its width steadily increased as it moved away from the straight part until it reached about 160 feet at the edge of the Avon. As for the discovery of Woodhenge, it was to be the point of departure for later research.

Crawford published several articles on his work and the circumstances that had prompted it. They attracted considerable attention because they showed how modern inventions were aiding study of the past. Since then, most books on Stonehenge have included an aerial view that gives a better idea of its overall design.

At about that same time, Dr. Herbert Thomas, petrographer to the geological survey, read before the

Society of Antiquaries an article that attracted still more attention. Its title was "The Source of the Stones of Stonehenge," and it was published in the *Antiquaries Journal* in July 1923. As the result of a thorough study of the bluestones and geological surveys conducted in Carmarthenshire, Dr. Thomas had situated the origin of those stones in the Prescelly Mountains in Pembrokeshire, southern Wales. As for the Altar Stone, it had come from a neighboring region, the Coheston Beds, near Milford Haven.

Till then, the bluestones were thought to have been brought into Wiltshire, from regions beyond Salisbury Plain, by glaciers of the Pleistocene epoch,* as stated by Professor Judd. Dr. Thomas, an eminent geologist, showed that such an origin was impossible. The incredible fact had to be accepted: The bluestones had been extracted 135 miles from Stonehenge! But aside from the enormous labor of transporting them over such a distance, the public was impressed by something else: a kind of half confirmation of Geoffrey of Monmouth's story. He had said that the stones of Stonehenge came from Ireland. Was there a particle of truth in that story, which had seemed to have been invented by medieval scribes? Wales is a considerable distance from Ireland, of course, but the idea that the stones had come from far away had turned out to be true, and many people wondered if the figure of Merlin the Enchanter did not represent the real master builder who had presided over the construction of Stonehenge.

I have visited the place from where the bluestones were taken. It is at the eastern end of the Prescelly Mountains, in the vicinity of a peak called Carn Meini, 1,195 feet high. Outcrops of spotted dolerite are plenti-

*This opinion was recently (1971) espoused again by a British geologist, G. A. Kellaway. One thing about "glacial solutions" has always puzzled me: The glaciers seem to have brought just enough stones to make the monument. If one asks what happened to the others, large and small, the answer given is that they disappeared long ago, having been used for building houses and roads. That reminds me of the accusation brought against treasure hunters to explain a completely empty dolmen.

ful here. Some of them have the shape of basalt columns. In some places one seems to be looking at the bluestones of Stonehenge, straight and ready to be detached. The Prescelly Mountains have a desolate look. Plant life is sparse, and stormy winds often blow, as in the vicinity of Land's End.

It has been said that this region was once considered to be holy, which would explain the fame of its stones among Neolithic peoples. The Prescelly Mountains have been called a "prehistoric Westminster." I saw no remains that would have supported such an opinion, but that proves nothing since I did not make a thorough study of the place. The region is rather rich in megalithic monuments. Three dolmens were called Arthur's Quoit, and that name may bring us back to Merlin. One of them is the impressive dolmen of Penter Ifan, between Cardigan and Newport. Its enormous slab, 10 feet above the ground, rests on two uprights with pointed ends.

While RAF planes were taking aerial photographs of Stonehenge, and Dr. Thomas was studying the origin of the bluestones, patient excavation work was being done inside the monument. After World War I, the Society of Antiquaries, encouraged by generous funding, resumed its activities. Its members decided to make extensive efforts at Stonehenge.

First of all, stones 1, 6, 7, and 30 of the Sarsen Circle, which were leaning dangerously, were placed upright again, and their bases were strengthened with concrete. This work, finished at the end of 1920, was given great publicity. In the year ending March 31, 1923, 37,450 people visited the monument, bringing in receipts of 1,196 pounds. The British public's fascination with Stonehenge began in that period. Within several years the annual number of visitors reached 100,000, and it has since gone far beyond that figure.

The excavation work was assigned to Lieutenant Colonel William Hawley, head of the Society of Antiquaries. It is impossible to read books and articles on Stonehenge written in the past thirty years without encountering Hawley's name again and again. What finds were made by that tireless excavator? He can be described as the great discoverer of the "holes" of Stonehenge, that is, nearly everything beneath the turf, the underground Stonehenge, invisible and unknown. He carried out most of his laborious task with the help of only one workman and, occasionally, students from Oxford and Cambridge. But he also had the valuable collaboration of R. S. Newall, who later took part in other excavations and related them to Hawley's. Newall wrote a little guidebook that was sold at the site of Stonehenge. Hundreds of copies of it were sold every day. (It now seems to have been replaced by R. J. C. Atkinson's *Stonehenge and Avebury.*)

One of Hawley's most important finds was the Aubrey Holes. As he and Newall were examining one of Aubrey's drawings, they had the idea of probing at places where small "cavities" were marked. Aubrey had been right, although he had drawn only five of those depressions, which were nearly indiscernible on the surface. And so the circle of fifty-six holes was found. Thirty of them were excavated immediately. As I said earlier, their contents consisted mostly of charred remains. Hawley believed they had been used for holding stones that formed a cromlech similar to the one at Avebury. That idea has since been completely abandoned.

In his research, Hawley used two simple tools: a tamper and a thin steel blade, sometimes a sword. The blade could be thrust down more easily at places where the chalk under the layer of soil had been hollowed out. When the tamper was dropped on the ground, it made a duller sound if the chalk under it had been disturbed. But Hawley's work was not limited to tests of this kind. He removed the topsoil from a third to a half of the total area of Stonehenge.

Among the holes he found, besides the Aubrey Holes, are the following:

1. The two concentric circles of Y and Z Holes.
2. Holes B and C on the axis of the Avenue.

3. The many post holes in the central part of the monument, on the Avenue, near the Heel Stone and at the entrance of the ditch and bank.

4. Four holes for stones between bluestones 33 and 34 and eight between 40 and 41.

5. The stone hole of station 92, with its inclined plane.

6. Holes F, G, and K on the circle of the Four Stations. Hawley did not think they had been used for holding stones, however; he believed they had been caused by the growth of bushes.

7. Three stone holes inside the monument, which he regarded as a possible extension of the Bluestone Horseshoe.

8. The stone hole of the Slaughter Stone's companion. Concerning this excavation, Hawley wrote:

> We came upon a very large hole roughly 10 feet in diameter by 6 1/2 feet deep which we gradually excavated. We found a coin of Claudius Gothicus in the upper layer, but nothing interesting until we reached the bottom, where two deerhorn picks were resting against the curved side. There can be no doubt that a large stone once stood in the hole.

I can here give only a brief sketch of that patient, persistent seeker's work. It was the subject of a long series of articles published under the title "Excavations at Stonehenge" in the *Antiquaries Journal* between 1920 and 1928. Hawley excavated half of the ditch and bank, from which he took, notably, 80 deer-antler picks, fragments of pottery from the Secondary Neolithic, and many cremated remains.

He also dug under the Slaughter Stone and found the bottle of port left there by Colt Hoare and Cunnington a hundred years earlier. He remarked regretfully that the quality of the cork had apparently not been as good as that of the wine. The bottle is now in the Salisbury Museum, along with some of the countless objects he gathered: stone mauls, flint tools, deer-antler picks, ox shoulderblades, pottery, and so on. He also discovered two graves and verified the course of the Avenue over a distance of 750 feet. He recognized that the ditches had been V-shaped, that they were practically parallel, and that the axis of the Avenue passed through the middle of the space between stones 1 and 30 of the Sarsen Circle.

His work has, of course, been criticized by his successors. He has been reproached for a certain lack of method, but he seems to have belonged to a category of researchers often encountered in the history of archaeology: He had a passion for excavating, not in order to draw conclusions—those he drew were timid, and he was afraid of criticism—but simply for the pleasure of finding ancient objects. He can be compared with Colt Hoare. He was the great discoverer of the underground Stonehenge that a visitor does not see, the "archaeological Stonehenge," and that was the main cause of the complaints made against him. He did not leave enough for researchers of the following generation.

During Hawley's work a remarkable book was published: *The Stones of Stonehenge* by E. H. Stone (London, 1924). Stone was an engineer, and he considered Stonehenge from a technical viewpoint. That was surely not the worst way to look at it, for while its builders showed an artistic sense, they also had practical techniques, and knowledge of them would be enlightening. Stone's book gives us valuable, precise information on the dimensions of the stones and the distances between them. It is one of the best aids for anyone who wants to draw an accurate plan of the monument. I myself have made use of it. Considering the results that had been obtained in his time, I regard his book as one of the best.

Stone was an advocate of Lockyer's theory. He presented Lockyer's work in great detail, with clear, simple diagrams. He believed the axis of the Avenue coincided with that of the monument, and this opinion led him into an impasse. He made models to show how the sarsen stones had been erected and a method that might have been used for putting the lintels in place. He also performed experiments, whose results are still valid, on the cutting and shaping of the stones. And his book is a rich treasury of details, legends, anecdotes, various opinions, drawings, diagrams, and dimensioned sketches.

Hawley finished his work in 1926, but Newall remained at the site. In 1929, with Reverend George Engleheart, he dug around fallen stone 36 of the Bluestone Circle. When he had taken away enough earth, he was able to see two mortise holes in the surface that had been in contact with the ground. This showed that, like stone 150, stone 36 had also been a lintel. If someone had shown the same curiosity as Newall and Engleheart earlier, many sterile arguments over whether there had been one or two bluestone trilithons would have been avoided.

From that time until the beginning of World War II, which necessarily interrupted all activity at Stonehenge, there were scarcely any noteworthy books except R. H. Cunnington's *Stonehenge and Its Date,* published in 1935. It deals with current problems in a concise, practical way. It also anticipates discoveries made after the war, notably on the original bluestone structure.

R. J. C. Atkinson

Hawley's excavations were not quite as decisive as had been hoped, but they suggested a great deal. Some specialists even thought they should be re-examined. New work was therefore done in 1953 and 1954 by three excellent archaeologists who wanted to make a basic reassessment of the problem of Stonehenge: Professor Stuart Piggott, who had defined the Wessex Culture in 1938; Dr. J. F. S. Stone, who had long been the director or archaeological research in the district; and R. J. C. Atkinson, professor of archaeology at the University College of South Wales at Monmouthshire, who was then engaged in a detailed study of the henge monument. The team was completed by Robert Newall, one of the men who knew the site best.

In 1947, J. F. S. Stone had opened a lengthwise trench in the Cursus. As the excavations showed, the Cursus had been made by the same method and with the same tools as the circular ditch and bank. Deer-antler picks identical with those discovered by Hawley were found. A stone chip of the same nature as the Altar Stone was also found. Close examination of the area between the Cursus and Stonehenge revealed the presence of many bluestone chips.

The first surprise, for the public, came after Aubrey Hole number 32 was excavated in 1950. Almost at the bottom of it was a piece of charcoal. There was nothing extraordinary about the discovery in itself, but Professor Libby, of Chicago, had just developed a method based on radioactivity that made it possible to date objects with organic matter in their composition. It is now well known as the carbon-14 method. By means of it, the piece of charcoal was dated at 1848 B.C., with a margin or error of plus or minus 275 years. Archaeological methods had led to a date in that same period: between 1900 and 1700 B.C.

I will not describe in detail the results of the great excavations of 1953–54. I will speak mainly of two unexpected discoveries. The first was the Q and R Holes, on either side of the present Bluestone Circle. The Q Holes were found first, between that circle and the Sarsen Circle. "In choosing this designation," Atkinson later wrote, "I had in mind John Aubrey's frequent use, as a marginal note in his unpublished MS. *Monumenta Britannica,* of the phrase 'quaere quot'—'inquire how many'—which seemed appropriate to the occasion."

But as excavation continued, it was seen that these holes were connected to others by small trenches. Each Q Hole outside the circle corresponded to an R Hole inside it. The pairs thus formed had the shape of a dumbbell. Examination of the holes showed clearly that stones had once been erected in them. Since all the chips found in them were bluestones, it was a bluestone structure that they had held. It was later dismantled so that the present structures could be built, after another had been tried in the Y and Z Holes.

A new phase of Stonehenge had been brought to light. In time, it lay between the henge monument and the sarsen structure. It seemed to prove that the whole monument had not been built in a single period. Unfortunately, the excavations were not carried far enough to uncover all of that second phase, but about half of the semicircle was studies. This part contained the area in which the Axis crossed the double circle; that is, the area containing stones 49 and 31 of the present circle. It was ascertained that the "dumbbells" on each side of the Axis had contained four or five stones instead of two, like all the others. Beginning with Stonehenge II, as Atkinson called it, the intention of orienting the monument toward sunrise at the summer solstice became apparent.

It is sometimes said that one tends to find what one is looking for, especially in archaeology. This may be true of many people, but it was not true of R. J. C. Atkinson one afternoon when he was preparing to photograph the inscription of Johannes de Ferre's name on the first upright of trilithon 53–54. The last thing he was expecting to see was a carving of a dagger on the upright, but that was what he saw. No one had ever reported its existence. Atkinson himself had passed upright 53 dozens of times without noticing the carving, and thousands of people before him had also looked at the surface of the stone without noticing anything. Yet the carving is there. Conditions were particularly favorable at the time when it was discovered, but those conditions had occurred countless times before, and the dagger could have been seen not only from inside the monument but also, with good eyesight, from the road, 260 feet away.* What a lesson for those who study things of the past!

*The presence of the inscription above the dagger must have been one reason why the dagger was not noticed sooner. The inscription, very regular and obvious, captures one's attention, and one does not think of looking above or below it.

The dagger carved on upright 53 is in a vertical position, point down. It has a triangular blade, a hilt with a pommel, and a total length of 11 inches, though the point seems to be prolonged to make a length of 12 or 12 1/2 inches. It was apparently carved "life-sized." It is of a type unknown in the second millennium B.C. not only in Great Britain but also in Western Europe. One of the most reasonable comparisons is with a dagger carved on a Mycenaean gravestone now in the National Museum at Athens. The carving shows a warrior driving a war chariot, armed with a dagger similar to the one at Stonehenge. The only difference is in the top of the pommel: It is rounded on the Mycenaean stone, flat on upright 53. The Mycenaean grave dates from about 1500 B.C. The carving might be later.*

The Aegean dagger is not the only carving at Stonehenge. After that discovery, more were made. Four axe heads, with their cutting edges turned upward, were found on upright 53. Traces of others could be seen, but their outlines were vague. A few days later, David Booth, the 10-year-old son of one of the men working on the excavations, found a larger group of axes on the outer surface of upright 4 in the Sarsen Circle. While Newall was taking cases of them, he found several others on the same stone, but they were less distinct. Three sharper ones were found on stone 3. Finally, various figures were discerned, notably on stones 23, 29, and 57, but it was not possible to make a reasonable guess about their meaning.

All these carvings except the dagger show a certain similarity to those found on some megalithic monuments in French Brittany. The axes have crescent-shaped edges. They seem to be reproductions of the bronze axes known to have been made in Ireland and distributed in England between 1600 and 1400 B.C.

In 1954 an interesting experiment was performed

*The length of the dagger carving given above is exactly the same as that of a dagger with a flanged tang, rather similar to the carving at Stonehenge, found at Mycenae. It is pictured in *Matériaux pour l'Histoire primitive et naturelle de l'Homme*, 1886, p. 11.

and broadcast as part of a BBC television program. The purpose was to show that the bluestones could have been transported by water. Three flat-bottomed boats were joined together by beams on which a concrete replica of a bluestone was laid. After being placed in the water near Salisbury, they were poled up the Avon by four schoolboys. Near Amesbury the concrete block was placed on a sledge and hauled to Stonehenge.

I have not seen the television program, but judging from photographs the concrete block seems a little small to replace a bluestone, at least one of the larger ones. It weighed about 3,000 pounds, whereas some bluestones weighed twice as much—not to mention the Altar Stone. One may wonder if boats like those used in the experiment but loaded with a stone like number 67, for example, could have floated on the Avon, whose water is always rather low.

On the basis of the work done in 1953–54, Atkinson wrote his *Stonehenge* (London, 1956), the most recent great book on the subject, aside from a rather special one to which I will devote an appendix. During the work, he said, a large part of his time was taken up with answering the many questions of visitors who watched the excavations. His book answers those questions. Its title might have been that of an article published by Atkinson in the magazine *Nature* in 1954: "Stonehenge in the Light of Recent Research," or of a booklet by J. F. S. Stone: "Stonehenge in the Light of Modern Research" (Salisbury, 1953).

One of the most interesting and important parts of Atkinson's book is Chapter 3, "The Sequence of Construction." Here is the summary he gives at the end of it, with the warning that the dates are "very approximate":

> 1900–1700 B.C. *Stonehenge I.* Construction of the bank, ditch, and Aubrey Holes. Erection of the Heel Stone, stones D and E, and the timber structure A. Inception and use of the cremation cemetery.

1700–1600 B.C. *Stonehenge II*. Transport of the bluestones from Pembrokeshire. Erection of the double circle in the Q and R Holes. Filling up of the east end of the ditch at the causeway. Digging and filling of the Heel Stone ditch. Construction of the Avenue. Dismantling of stones D and E and timber structure A. Possible erection of stones B and C.

1500 B.C. *Stonehenge IIIa*. Transport of the sarsen stones from near Marlborough. Dismantling of the double circle of bluestones. Erection of the sarsen trilithons, circle, Station Stones, and the Slaughter Stone and its companion. Carvings executed on the stones.

1500–1400 B.C. *Stonehenge IIIb*. Tooling and erection of stones of the dressed bluestone setting. Digging and abandonment of the Y and Z Holes.

1400 B.C. *Stonehenge IIIc*. Dismantling of the dressed bluestone setting. Re-erection of these and the remaining bluestones in the present circle and horseshoe.

A.D. 50–400 Possibly some deliberate destruction of the stones.

Some restoration work was undertaken in 1957. Upright 22 of the Sarsen Circle, lintel 122, and trilithon 57–58, which had fallen on January 3, 1797, were put back in place. As with other stones that had been re-erected, concrete was poured into their foundations, so that they now have solid bases. Every effort was made to assure that these stones were placed in their original positions.

We can only hope that there will be further restoration. Three other uprights of the Sarsen Circle, 12, 14, and 25, could be put back in place, along with a certain number of bluestones. But above all there is the Great Trilithon. Although it is broken in two, upright 55 could be re-erected after its pieces were joined by means of steel spikes. That would help to solve one of the most puzzling problems of Stonehenge, for one feature of the monument is that a restoration cannot fail to be authentic: There is only one way to re-erect an upright since its foundation hole still exists.

I have visited Stonehenge before and after the most recent work on it. Its appearance has changed for the better. It now seems much less chaotic, and the restored trilithon is truly impressive. But a more complete restoration might be desirable on a scientific level. The surfaces of stones in contact with the ground may bring revelations, as has happened in the past. Let us also recall the carvings. Others may be discovered on surfaces that are now invisible, and who can foresee what they might teach us? Finally, the re-erection of other uprights would clear more ground for future excavations.

During the restoration work, a few additional excavations were made. The most important result was the discovery, or confirmation, that the double circle of bluestones in the Q and R Holes had never been finished. It also became possible to gain a more precise idea of the central bluestone structure built during the Stonehenge IIIb period.

Atkinson took account of these discoveries in *Stonehenge and Avebury*, a booklet of about twenty pages, including the excellent illustrations, published in 1959. It is still the best booklet on the monument itself and the prehistory of Wiltshire. Finally, Atkinson's *Stonehenge* was republished by Pelican Books in 1960. It includes an appendix in which he describes the results of work done at Stonehenge in 1956 and 1958.

PART THREE

The Construction of Stonehenge

The Henge Monument

The earthworks that composed the henge monument, or original Stonehenge monument, must not have presented any difficulties. Deer-antler picks and shovels made from ox shoulderblades were strong enough to dig into the chalk. When necessary, fire-hardened stakes were driven into the chalk, chunks of it were pried loose, and digging was completed with picks and shovels. The excavated material used for building the bank beside the ditch may have been removed by means of baskets passed from hand to hand. In short, construction of the earthworks does not seem to have been beyond the technical means of people living in that place about four thousand years ago.

Judging from the number of enclosures, camps, and grave mounds, some of which required immense movements of earth, those people were great builders of earthworks. The best example is the extraordinary monument of Silbury Hill, less than a mile south of Avebury. It has the shape of an enormous truncated cone, with a height of about 160 feet and a base diameter of about 560. Its purpose is unknown. The regularity of its shape suggests that it was built by highly skilled workers, and it shows what could be done by the people of that time. According to British

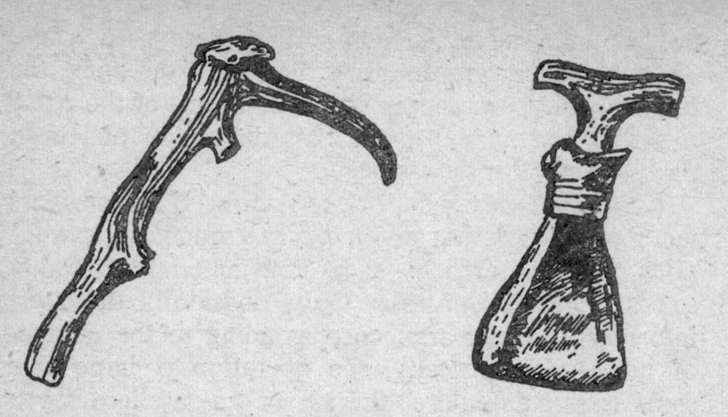

FIGURE 24—Tools used by the builders of the henge monument.

archaeologists, however, Silbury Hill was built several centuries after the original Stonehenge monument.

As far as we can judge now, the bank formed a fairly regular circle. There is still a circle with a diameter of 320 feet inside the bank, whose edges are about 8 feet apart. If there is an error, it is thus less than one-fortieth, which is remarkable for a structure that has undergone so many variations through the centuries. Moreover, the regularity of the ditch and bank appears clearly in aerial photographs.

This shows that the earliest Stonehenge builders knew how to lay out a circle on the ground, probably by means of a thong attached to a post at one end, with a wooden scriber at the other. The procedure seems very simple at first but less so if we put ourselves in the builders' place, assuming, of course, that they wanted to give their bank as regular a circular shape as possible.

As we have seen, the ditch had no other purpose than supplying material for the bank. The earth taken from it was dumped along its inner edge. The builders could therefore not have started by drawing the circle of the bank on the ground. They had to draw the circle of the ditch and dig around it, staying as close to it as possible. When the digging had been finished, the bank must have had a very irregular shape that had to be evened out. The thong and scriber were used again. The scriber was moved along the top of the bank, the thong having been shortened to the radius of the circle to be formed by the bank. This dimension had been decided before work was begun.

Laying out the circle for the Aubrey Holes was less laborious. The builders worked at ground level, without being hampered by excavated material. But what seems rather extraordinary is the division of the circle into fifty-six equal arcs, corresponding to the number of holes. Geometrically, the operation is impossible since it would require division of an arc into seven equal parts. But here again we should not look for a precision that was probably not intended by the builders. Although the Aubrey Holes are positioned on the circle at fairly regular intervals, their nature makes exact verification impossible.

Even so, the relative regularity of their spacing shows that they were not positioned at random. If a method of approximation was used, it proceeded from a certain base, which may have been a division of the circle into four quadrants. Such a division seems easy to us, but let us again imagine people on Salisbury Plain four thousand years ago, with no instruments but leather thongs and wooden stakes. We would have to assume that, given a straight line, a diameter, for example, they knew how to draw a line perpendicular to it at its center. This would involve only elementary notions of geometry, but it would presuppose that a "leap" into pure science and abstraction had been made at that time and place, which seems to me unlikely on the part of people of the Secondary Neolithic.

Instead of a purely geometrical method, I prefer to think of what might be called a more natural procedure. Neolithic people were surely familiar with the idea of the four cardinal points. Dividing a circle into four equal parts in accordance with the directions given by those points is a possibility that can reasonably be considered. It seems that the diameter of Aubrey Holes 20 and 48 gives the north-south direction, that of 6 and 34 the east-west direction. That, at least, is what can be deduced from the best plans of Stonehenge. When four quadrants had been obtained, each of them could have been divided into two equal parts, but I do not believe the builders knew how to bisect an angle.

They may have proceeded by first planting small stakes close enough together to outline the curve. A thong pressed against the stakes would give the length of the arc, and, of course, half the length of the thong would divide the arc into two equal parts. Holes could be dug at each of the eight points dividing the circle into eight equal parts, and then six holes, spaced as evenly as possible by approximation, could be dug in each of the intervals between these points, giving a total of fifty-six. Two pairs of opposite holes, 52–27 and 41–13, seem to have marked diameters dividing the first four quadrants into two equal parts. And one of the openings in the ditch and bank is south of its center, while the other is almost directly northeast of it. This would partially confirm the method described above.

The task would have been less complicated if sixty-four holes had been dug instead of fifty-six. Successive bisections would have made the layout easier. We may therefore assume that the number 56 had a special meaning to the builders, though we cannot say anything on the subject with certainty.*

It would be interesting to know if the builders used a unit of length. The diameter of the bank was certainly not determined by guesswork since it had to be found again after the ditch had been dug. The same must have been true of the circle on which the Aubrey Holes were placed. What was that unit? Did it have a physical standard? Did it simply correspond to the average length of a man's stride? Comparisons with

*An American astronomer, Gerald Hawkins, believes that the fifty-six Aubrey Holes served as a protractor and were used for predicting eclipses! That opinion seems rather rash to me. (See Appendix 3.)

other henge monuments might shed light on this problem, which was considered by Stukeley and Petrie.

Petrie proposed a cubit of Phoenician origin with a length of 22.5 inches. Applied to the ditch and bank, it gave the following results:

Inner edge of the bank:
3,595 inches (299 feet 7 inches) ÷ 22.5 = 160 units

Junction of the bank and the ditch:
4,044 inches (337 feet) ÷ 22.5 = 180 units

Outer edge of the ditch:
4,488 inches (374 feet) ÷ 22.5 = 200 units

The proposed unit thus tallied with the assumed dimensions of the ditch and bank, but in Petrie's time the Aubrey Holes had not yet been rediscovered. They form, if not a perfect circle, at least one that is easier to determine. But the cubit of 22.5 inches does not apply to the diameter of that circle: 3,435 inches (286 feet 3 inches) ÷ 22.5 = 152.67 units. Nor does it apply to the circumference or the spaces between the holes.

Furthermore, it is unlikely that the builders took the three dimensions indicated above. They probably had only two: a provisional one for laying out the perimeter of the excavation and a definitive one for marking the top of the circular bank. As for the Druidic cubit of 20.8 inches proposed by Stukeley, it is also not adapted to the diameter of the Aubrey Holes.

In the preceding discussion I have not considered the possibility of external influences. If such influences could be proved, the henge monument would be viewed in a different way. For example, instead of fixing the diameter of the circle at the outset, the builders might have used its circumference, which would imply that they knew a value of pi. That is not absolutely impossible, but it would be hard to demonstrate, and it would take us far beyond Salisbury Plain.

The Heel Stone and the Avenue

According to Atkinson, the Heel Stone dates from the same time as the henge monument. That seems rather strange to me. The Heel Stone, isolated from the other stones of Stonehenge, is a simple menhir. It is hard to explain its association with the ditch and bank and the circle of Aubrey Holes. I do not know if such an association is frequent in henge monuments, but the one at Stonehenge seems noteworthy. Moreover, the Heel Stone is a sarsen, and the nearest source of sarsens is in the Marlborough Downs, near Avebury. If Atkinson is right, then, a sarsen block had already been brought from that distance three or four centuries before the sarsen structure was built.

The Heel Stone and its ditch and bank show a certain similarity to stations 92 and 94, which were originally composed of a standing stone surrounded by a small ditch. That pattern seems to have been applied to the untooled or roughly tooled sarsen stones, and as I have said, it was applied with obvious disregard of earlier earthworks. If the Heel Stone is from the same time as the henge monument, we must assume that its circular ditch was dug after construction of the Avenue, since it cuts almost completely across it, leaving only about six feet between itself and the bank. If we accept Atkinson's sequence, it was made more than a hundred years after the Heel Stone was erected.

But if the Heel Stone is earlier than the Avenue, its location in relation to the latter is particularly surprising. It is not on its axis, and it seems odd that it was not moved when the Avenue was built. It must have been a rather troublesome obstacle, especially if the Avenue was used for transporting the stones of the monument.

One interesting possibility: The center of the henge monument and the left side of the Heel Stone (what I will later call point H) seem to form a straight line parallel to the axis of the Avenue.

I will later discuss the place that the Heel Stone

occupies in the plan of the sarsen structure. It was erected in the same way as countless other standing stones found in many parts of the world. A hole was dug with one side forming an inclined plane. The stone was slid into it, and the effort then required to lift it to a vertical position was relatively small. The main problem lay in transporting it from its place of origin to its final location. I will come back to that point in relation to the sarsen structure.

The actual construction of the Avenue—digging the ditches and making banks of the earth removed from them—must not have presented any difficulties. But its straightness is remarkable. I know of no other prehistoric work comparable to it: such a long, straight earthwork at ground level. We may conclude that the builders knew how to determine two parallel alignments, probably by staking out the axis and making perpendicular lines on either side of it to mark the edges of the road.

The Avenue is aligned in the direction of sunrise at the summer solstice. Its center line was the famous Axis about which there has been so much discussion. It was probably marked by two stones, now gone, in the middle of the Avenue near the opening in the ditch and bank (B and C in Figure 4). There had to be some sort of physical marker if sunrise was to be observed accurately.

Transport of the Bluestones

This is a question that has caused a great deal of ink to flow. Nearly everyone now agrees that the bluestones came from southern Wales, but there is considerable difference of opinion with regard to the route followed from Pembrokeshire to Salisbury Plain. In Figure 25 I have shown five routes, numbered I through V, chosen from among those most often proposed. Let us first examine the entirely overland route (Route I).

I will say at the outset that it is the least likely. The distance from the Prescelly Mountains to Stone-

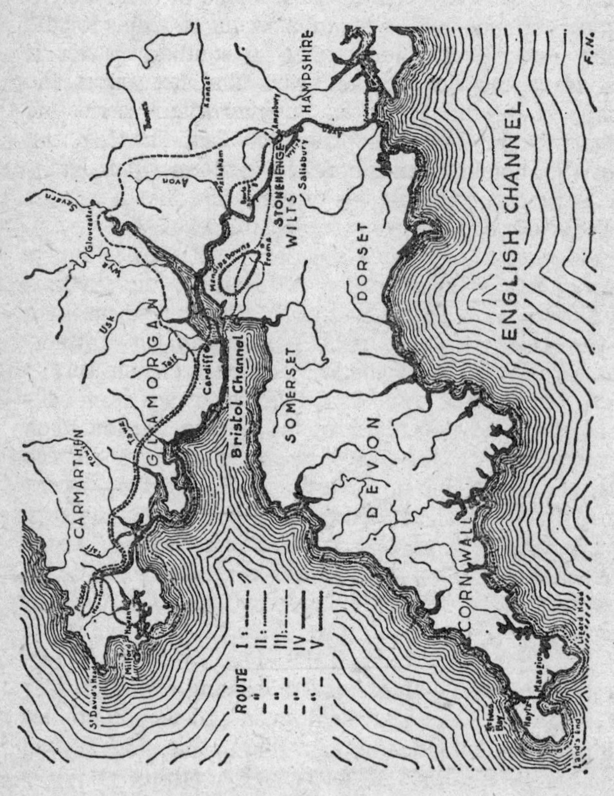

FIGURE 25—Transport of the bluestones.

henge, as the crow flies, is about 135 miles. It would have been close to 200 miles with the detour required to avoid the Bristol Channel, crossing the Severn near Gloucester. But distance would not have been the major obstacle. The lay of the land is such that the transporters would have been foolish to take that route. They had to move about eighty stones, some of them weighing more than 4 tons, with a maximum of 7 tons for the Altar Stone. The whole region in southern Wales is full of valleys and coastal rivers that cut across the proposed route. It is an uninterrupted series of obstacles. The Towy, the Tawe, the Taff, the Usk, and the Wye, notably, cause crossing problems. It is likely that after making rafts for crossing the first river, the transporters would have preferred the sea route.

Mixed routes have also been proposed. For example: overland from the Prescelly Mountains to the environs of Cardiff, then across the Bristol Channel, then along the Bristol Avon to a point downstream from Malksham, then overland again to Stonehenge (Route II).

Another mixed route is as follows: by sea from Milford Haven or the mouth of the Taff to Weston, then overland along the ridge road of Mendip Downs (Route III). This hypothesis is supported to some extent by the fact that in 1801 William Cunnington found a block of rhyolite in the Bowles Barrow, about 12 miles from Stonehenge.* This discovery can also be used in favor of the two other mixed routes. From that region to Stonehenge, all three could easily be merged.

The third mixed route is the same by sea as the one described above, but instead of passing overland near Weston it goes up the Bristol Avon and then continues almost entirely along rivers: the Frome, the Wylye, and the Hampshire Avon to Amesbury (Route IV).

Finally, the route that seems to be most widely accepted is almost exclusively by sea, from Milford Haven to Christchurch, with or without a rounding of Land's

*I have already referred to this find. The block, which weighs a ton, is now in the Salisbury Museum. Its size seems small to me for such a weight.

End (Route V). An embarkation at Milford Haven has been more or less definitively accepted since the origin of the Altar Stone was found to be in the Cohes-ton Beds, near Milford Haven. Furthermore, sailing around St. David's Head is very dangerous, and it would have been natural to avoid it since the stones had to be brought to the shore in any case. Sailing along the southern shore of Wales, then along the shores of Somerset, Devon, and Cornwall, would have brought the boats to St. Ives Bay.

From there, opinion is divided. Some believe that Land's End was rounded; others feel that this passage was also too dangerous for heavily laden boats and that it was avoided either by unloading the boats at Hayle, taking them around St. David's Head empty and transporting the stones overland to Marazion, or by dragging both the boats and the stones to Marazion. This seems impractical, although examples of similar procedures can be found.

I prefer to assume that the loaded boats rounded St. David's Head. The people of that period seem to have been excellent sailors who did not hesitate to travel far from shore, if only to avoid the risk of being thrown against it. The propagation of the megalithic idea clearly shows this. It is therefore possible that in the period we are considering there were good pilots thoroughly familiar with the coasts and dangerous passages. That is why I believe that the transporters went by sea from Milford Haven to the mouth of the Avon. By going up the Avon to Amesbury, they brought the bluestones to within 2 miles of Stonehenge.

We know nothing about the nature of the boats used. Were they propelled by oars or sails? Probably by both. We are no better informed on their size and shape. If each of them carried only one stone, they must have been quite light for confronting the sea; if each of them carried several stones, they had to be altered, or others had to be used, for going up the Avon since it would have been too shallow for large vessels, assuming that it was essentially the same as it is today.

Although prehistoric sea travel is proved by many facts, we still know little about it, probably because few discoveries have been made in that area. We do not even know much more about the vessels of certain seafaring peoples such as the Phoenicians and Cretans, for example. Perhaps underwater archaeology, which is still a young science, will bring us the elements we lack. We know only that at the time when the bluestones were transported, vessels on the Nile carried loads of obelisks weighing several hundred tons.

Did an army from Salisbury Plain go into the Prescelly Mountains to bring back the bluestones, or did a migratory people from that region go to settle in the vicinity of Stonehenge, bringing their sacred stones with them? The first possibility is the one generally accepted. It tallies with what existed at Stonehenge before the second phase and with Geoffrey of Monmouth's legend.

If that assumption is correct, what route was followed on the outward journey? Did the transporters build boats on the shore of the English Channel to take them to the Prescelly Mountains by sea? If they first traveled overland and then returned by sea, they must have had good geographical knowledge because before coming back with the stones, they first had to reach them. Traders in axes or tin may have had something to do with it, but a large-scale expedition would seem to have been involved.

Transporting 300 tons of stone from Pembrokeshire to Stonehenge was an amazing feat, especially in the context of Western Europe in about 1500 B.C. It is rightly regarded as one of the most striking facts about Stonehenge. It represents such a sum of efforts, knowledge, skill, and courage that only a religious motive could have brought it about.

Why were those famous bluestones brought from so far away? According to Geoffrey of Monmouth's legend, they had curative powers, but is that enough to explain such an expedition? It is said that they may have had a special holiness. If so, it is strange that their holiness was recognized only by people living in the vicinity of Stonehenge. As far as I know, there is no other monument made of those same stones anywhere else in Great Britain outside of Wales.

The transport of the bluestones has another unusual aspect. Until that time, large movements of people had been one-way journeys, migrations. A tribe left one area to settle in another, with no intention of returning. But in order to bring the bluestones to Stonehenge, a large number of people, undoubtedly several thousand, left the place where they lived and came back to it after traveling 400 miles. Imagine what such an expedition involved! And it was accomplished by people about whom we know so little that we identify them by the utensils they used for drinking!

The bluestones were transported during the period of the megalithic monuments. The builders of those monuments never hesitated to go considerable distances for the materials they needed. The slabs of the dolmen at Saint-Fort-sur-le-Né, in the Charente department of France, were taken from 19 miles away; those of the dolmen at Moulins, in the Indre department, from 22 miles away; and the granite in the covered passage at Soto, in Andalusia, from 24 miles away. There are other examples. But they are comparable only to the sarsen stones of Stonehenge; the builders brought stones from far away only because there was no nearer source.

That is not true of the bluestones. Between Salisbury Plain and Pembrokeshire there are outcrops of rocks that could have been used for making a cromlech. Stonehenge is a unique case, even among monuments made of untooled stones. Blocks of dolerite and rhyolite from the Prescelly Mountains therefore had great value to the people of Salisbury Plain—and only to them, it seems. How did they come to attribute that value to them? We do not know. Commercial exchanges between two such distant regions could be, at best, only a partial explanation.

Whatever the reason behind it, and whatever the route it followed, the transport of the bluestones was an extraordinary feat. If it had been accomplished in archaic Greece, we might have a third Homeric epic.

Transport of the Sarsen Stones

The source of the sarsen stones of Stonehenge has been situated at about 19 miles north of the monument, in the vicinity of Avebury. The stones of the gigantic cromlech that still surrounds part of Avebury are sarsens. But one might ask if there was not once a nearer source, now exhausted, since the greywethers do not have the tabular shape of the Stonehenge uprights. The answer to that question might be dubious if the stones of the Avebury cromlech were not like those of Stonehenge, except that they are untooled. The general opinion is that they all came from the same source.

If that source was in the Marlborough Downs north of the Kennet River, between Avebury and Marlborough, the stones had to be taken across the river, probably by means of a floating bridge. Then, to avoid the slopes of the right bank of the Kennet Valley, the transporters went southwest, toward Devizes. Near Bishops Cannings they turned south to cross the broad Vale of Pewsey. From there, they probably followed an ancient road between Devizes and Salisbury. That road is now closed to the public by the military camps it crosses. The main difficulty lay in climbing the steep slopes of the right bank of the Vale of Pewsey. The transporters may either have taken a winding route to diminish the slope, or gone around the heights to the west. The vanished branch of the Avenue, which in the past was seen extending toward the Cursus, may have been part of a road made for transporting the sarsen stones.

Whatever the route that was followed, the difficulties must have been enormous. In my opinion, they were greater than those involved in transporting the bluestones. First of all, the stones had to be lifted out of the ground and placed on rollers. This might have been done by means of log levers, using stones or other logs as fulcrums. To lift one end of a 30-ton stone similar to

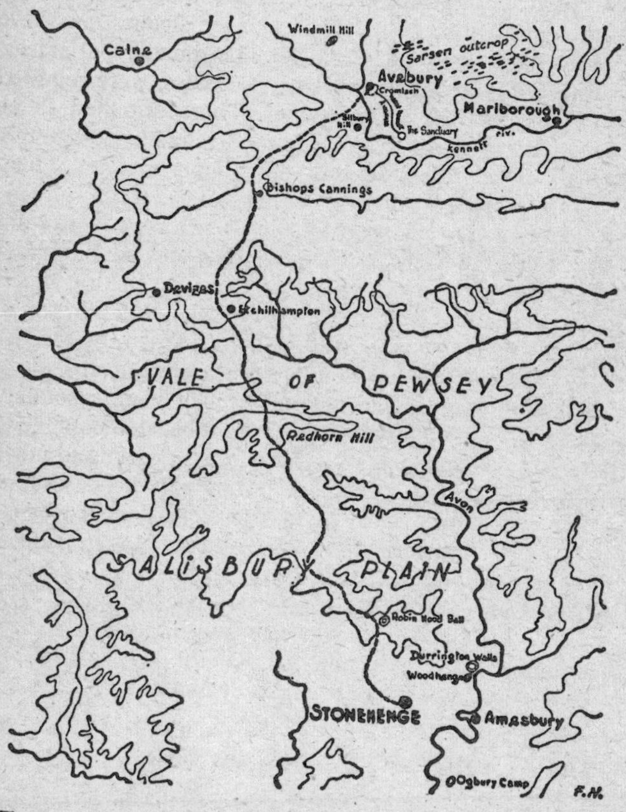

FIGURE 26—Transport of the sarsen stones according to R.J.C. Atkinson.

the sarsens, a force of 2,600 to 2,800 pounds must be exerted on levers 7 to 10 feet long. Twenty men would be sufficient.

Once they were on rollers, the stones were probably placed on sledges and dragged across the ground with ropes. A road may have been made along the whole route, and at steep places the loaded sledges may have been placed on rollers. It has been estimated that at least fifteen hundred men, working five years, were required to transport the sarsen stones. There also had to be men to cut down trees, make and repair ropes, supply food for the other workers, and so on. We cannot help thinking of an organized, hierarchical society.

Essentially, transporting the sarsen stones was not very different from transporting the stones used in building other monuments in ancient and prehistoric times. Whether we consider the stones of the Great Pyramid, the 150-ton slab of the Antequera dolmen, or the uprights of the Great Trilithon at Stonehenge, the problem is the same. Distance and weight were secondary matters, in my opinion. As soon as it became possible to move a 50-ton stone a few feet, it was possible to move dozens of them many miles. It was only a question of time and labor. The real problem consisted first in inventing methods of lifting and transporting the stones, then in assembling a large enough group of men, using force or persuasion to carry out the task. The essential elements, then, were an organized society and a technology. They must both have existed in Western Europe in the second millennium B.C.

The Tooling of the Sarsen Stones

The sarsen stones, which compose the most impressive structure of Stonehenge, were all tooled to some extent, except for the Heel Stone. To the best of my knowledge, Stonehenge is the only example of a complete prehistoric structure whose stones were not untooled. We must not exaggerate, however. The tooling of the Stonehenge stones is rather uneven. There are some fine specimens, such as upright 56, stone 16, the lintel of trilithon 53–54, and those of the Sarsen Circle, but most of the others have very irregular surfaces and edges or are only half tooled. Were the builders unwilling to do the great work that more complete shaping would have required? This unfinished aspect of the monument appears only when it is examined in detail. Taken together, the sarsen uprights give a good impression of regularity; moreover, they were roughly tooled to produce that impression.

The first rough tooling must have been done at the place of extraction to avoid transporting useless weight. The sarsen stones used in the structure are mostly tabular blocks formed from broad slabs with two parallel surfaces, which came from sandstone beds of uniform thickness. Good examples are found in the Avebury cromlech and the Kennet Avenue, in which the stones in their natural state often have the shape of a rectangle or a rhombus.

Preliminary cutting therefore seems to have taken place before the stones were transported. It may have been done by splitting, using natural cracks corresponding to the desired dimensions. Where no such cracks existed, they may have been created to enable wooden wedges to be driven in. Or the operation may have been reduced to a series of holes, more or less closely spaced, as was apparently done in French Brittany to cut the slabs of dolmens. The wedges were soaked with water, and the swelling of the wood split the stone.

Another method that may have been used consisted in cutting grooves outlining the desired shape, heating the stone along them, and then pouring cold water into them. The sudden cooling of the stone caused internal tension that was strong enough to break it if, at the same time, men pounded it with mauls on both sides of the groove. In the seventeenth and eighteenth centuries, according to Aubrey and Stukeley, Avebury peasants still used this method for breaking up stones from the cromlech. But the stones of Stonehenge show no trace of the procedures described above.

When they had been reduced to the required dimensions and transported to the site, the stones were tooled to give them a flat surface if they did not already have one. This tooling was done before the uprights were erected since some of them have tooled surfaces on their buried parts. British archaeologists describe the process as follows. First, lengthwise grooves 8 to 10 inches wide were made in the stone with heavy sarsen mauls. (Such grooves are clearly visible in the fallen upright of trilithon 59–60.) Then the ridges between the grooves were pounded away until the surface was flat.

It was a very slow process requiring many workers and much time. The heavy mauls had the size of a soccer ball, the smallest ones that of an orange. Some of them have been found in the holes of uprights, where they were placed to strengthen the foundations. Experiments using the same method and tools have shown it was possible to do the work in that way. E. H. Stone showed that a man could remove about 6 cubic inches of stone in an hour, in the form of dust, and Atkinson made the following calculation: Assuming that an average thickness of 2 inches was removed, the total volume was 3 million cubic inches. With fifty men working ten hours a day, seven days a week, the job would have taken two years and nine months. And this was only for the surfaces of the uprights and lintels.

At least as much time was probably required to form tenons on top of the uprights by removing the stone from around them and to form mortises and V-shaped joints in the lintels. According to British authors, the same methods and tools were used for this work. That seems possible for the mortises and tenons but more questionable for the V-shaped joints. How could the angles and straight lines of those joints have been made with spherical mauls? Were other tools used? If so, none of them has been discovered unless the many pieces of flint found in excavations were used for that purpose.

The above description also applies to the tooling of the bluestones in the horseshoe, which were given the shape of small obelisks.

By now the reader may have wondered if metal was used. The answer is simple. Copper and bronze were the only metals known during that period; iron did not appear until several centuries later. Those metals were rare. They were used only for making ornaments and weapons. They were the property of a privileged class whose members probably had no desire to sacrifice them for tools. And in any case copper or bronze tools would quickly have been dulled by stone as hard as sarsen. At that time, the best material for shaping stone was stone itself.

The Double Bluestone Circles

According to British scientists, as we have seen, the stone structure was to have begun with a double bluestone circle marked out by the Q and R Holes inside the Sarsen Circle. That is what Atkinson calls Stonehenge II (Figure 10). But it was never finished. Strangely enough, there was a later attempt to make a similar double circle inside the monument, in the Y and Z Holes, but again the project was abandoned. Finally, there were the figures now formed by the bluestones: a circle and a horseshoe.

Why were the first two projects abandoned? A great catastrophe, such as an epidemic or a war, has been suggested, particularly with regard to the double circle of the Y and Z Holes. It is possible in that case, but it seems less likely in the case of the Q and R Holes.

Why should that structure have been abandoned when it was more than half finished? The stones were erected as the holes were dug. Then the erecting of the stones and the digging of the holes were both stopped at the same time. We may conclude that the holes were not all dug at once after their positions had been laid out on the ground. The center of the structure therefore had to be always available, so that the builders could take radii, unless the holes had been marked with posts. That center must have been indicated by a small wooden stake.

The double circle of the Q and R Holes was thus abandoned in the midst of its construction. Had the builders come to realize that, in spite of their special nature, those stones were not large enough for a temple worthy of the sun god? Was the double circle originally included in the final plan, then dismantled because it proved to be a hindrance?

This seems likely because the Stonehenge builders apparently always came up against major difficulties in making several similar and concentric structures, one outside another. If the outline of the structure on the ground was shallow, it was quickly wiped away by the passage of stones on rollers; if it was deep, it interfered with moving the stones. Even if stakes were used to mark the positions of the stones, they might be moved by the heavy masses that had to pass close to them. Once a circle had been built, it was hard to build another one outside it. It could be done, provided it was possible to find the center again, but the second circle would not be as precise as the first. That was what happened with the present horseshoe. Abandonment of the double circle in the Q and R Holes would then be justified. Even without stones in them, the holes would have created a serious obstacle to erection of the sarsens because clear, level ground was needed. But why should the double circle have been begun?

At first, there was probably no intention of building a sarsen structure. A solar temple was planned since the direction of sunrise at the summer solstice was marked in the double circle of the Q and R Holes, but the possibility of a more grandiose temple had not yet come to light—unless that bluestone structure was only a first attempt, made after the sarsens had been erected. Future research may indicate whether that hypothesis is well founded or not. In any case, it is likely that not much time went by between the abandonment of the double circle and the beginning of work on the great Stonehenge.

We cannot say much about the design of the double circle. It was never completed, and it consists of nothing but holes, so we cannot count on precise measurements. To the best of my knowledge, no exact plan of it has been published. The diameter of the R Hole circle was 74 feet, and that of the Q Hole circle was 86 feet. I do not believe that two concentric circles were laid out, rather an average circle of 80 feet, the stones arranged in pairs on either side of it, on a single radius.

Nor can we say anything about an elliptical bluestone structure that may have been built at the center of the monument. In it may have been included the bluestone trilithons, joined uprights 66 and 68, and the Altar Stone standing vertically. Here again, no exact plan of those holes has been published, or at least I know of none, and it would be hazardous to attempt any theory on the subject. It seems better to wait for future research before forming an opinion.

But, anticipating the chronological order of the work, I will say a few words on the double circle of the Y and Z Holes. Having been laid out after the sarsens were erected, those holes necessarily formed very irregular figures, as we have seen. Their layout shows such clumsiness, even allowing for the hindrance created by the trilithons, that it is easy to believe the great architect was not there to guide the work. Such circles were unworthy of existing around the great Stonehenge, and the project was rightly abandoned.

The Great Stonehenge

After the ground had been leveled, the builders' first task must have been to determine the axis of the monument. That axis would give it its center and orientation. How was its orientation toward sunrise at the summer solstice obtained? It might seem to be a very simple procedure, but not to anyone who repeats it at the site, especially if he wants to achieve a certain accuracy.

Practically speaking, we cannot recreate the exact conditions of the operation since we know in advance not only the day when the phenomenon will occur but also the exact moment and even the point on the horizon if we know the geographical coordinates of the place. Even with that knowledge, however, we soon realize that the observer's position is the most important factor and that it must always be the same. If, for example, a telescope is permanently fixed so that it is aimed at a certain point, and if an observer looks through it to watch for sunrise at that point, he cannot stand anywhere but behind the eyepiece. Whoever he is, whatever his attitude, whichever eye he uses, he will always see the sun at that point on the same date.

If we replace the telescope with a row of stones or posts, the result will be the same. What we need is a device independent of the observer, permanently aimed at a certain point. And that device must have at least two markers, comparable to the front and rear sights of a rifle.

But no such system exists inside the monument. If, as has been supposed, the observer stood behind the Great Trilithon, there was nothing to impose a fixed position on his gaze unless there were markers outside, in the direction of the Slaughter Stone or the Avenue, but then the only means of fixing the summer solstice would have been outside the monument, which would have been strange for a temple dedicated to the sun god. It is more likely that at least one marker existed inside the monument, where, to use an expression applied to the solar temples of the Incas, "the sun had been chained to a pillar."*

If that was the case, the line of sight must have gone through the monument and the fixed point must have been outside it. And if we imagine the empty area ready to receive stones, we are obliged to think of an axis running through the structure. Before beginning work, then, the builders laid out a line that crossed the site and had a marker at each end. That line extended toward the point on the horizon where the sun rose at the summer solstice, a direction that had already been approximately determined with the double circle of bluestones. The two markers, or others later placed on the same line, imposed a specific position on any observer.

I will give the name of point H to the first marker

*To the worshipers, this meant that the priests had marked the extreme limits of the sun's advance. It had to run its course between two limits. It therefore seemed to obey the priests, or at least grant their prayers, when they asked it not to go away, to come back and light the world for mankind.

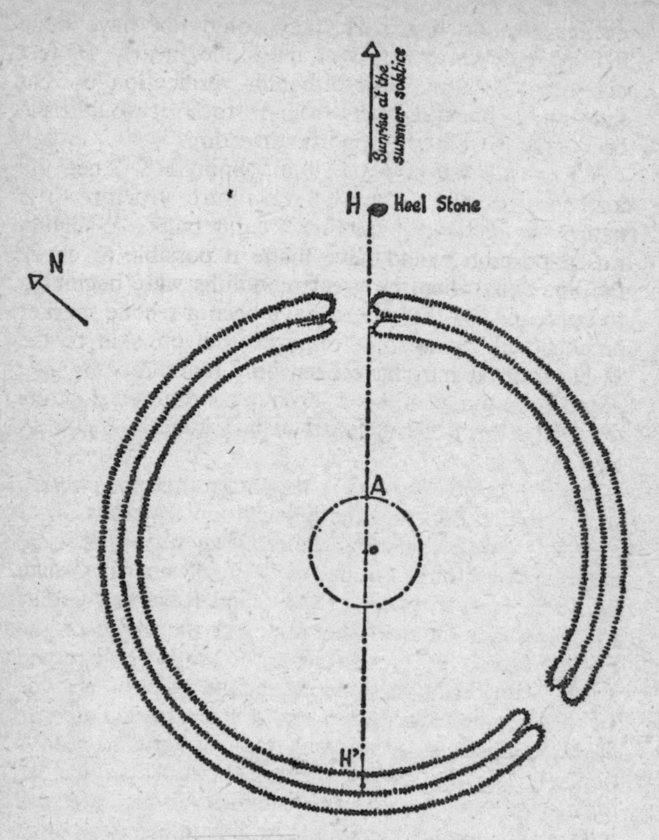

FIGURE 27—Line H'H and the theoretical sarsen circle.

on the axis. (See Figure 27.) It coincided with the left side of the Heel Stone, which provided an ideal support. Because of its size, it was not in danger of being shifted or removed by the coming and going of hundreds of workers or the passage of heavy stones on rollers. But one might wonder why the marker was not placed on the top of the Heel Stone rather than on its side. That would have been less practical. Calling the second marker H′, we can see that if the builders had to measure distances along line H′H, they could not have done it if H had been on top of the stone, nearly 16 feet above the ground. And although verification of that line would have been easy from H′ to H, it would have been impossible in the opposite direction.

Where are we now to situate point H′? Since the axis had to cross the site of the future structure, it is natural to imagine it on the circular bank. A slightly raised position would have made it possible to check the line even when the great monoliths were beginning to approach. So there must have been a second marker on the bank, at a point opposite the left side of the Heel Stone. It may have been only temporary. It may also have been at ground level, the observer standing on the bank. The following would seem to support this.

Many researchers have believed that there was once a stone directly opposite the Heel Stone at point H′, or at least very close to it. This idea was expressed, notably, by John Smith (1771), Richard Gough (1789), Henry Browne (1823), and Reverend Gidley (1873). They situated the stone on the circle of the Four Stations. In 1893 Professor J. W. Judd discerned a small mound at that place and the base of a stone 10 inches above the surface. He gave its orientation as 51 degrees west of south, which corresponds to a position opposite the Heel Stone. Later, Lockyer did no further research on the subject even though he was interested in it and simply cited the fruitless work done at the turn of the century by Penrose, Howard Payn, and Sir Edmund Entrobus. I am not aware of any research that has been done since then. A solution to the problem would have a certain interest, although there is nothing surprising about the present absence of a marker at that place.

Line H′H determined the monument's axis of symmetry. Its end points were outside the construction area and could therefore not interfere with the movement of stones or be affected by it. It could always be found at any stage of construction and under all circumstances. The distance from point H′ to point H is about 423 feet. From its center, the theoretical line of the Sarsen Circle could be drawn.

But before laying out that circle on the ground, let us consider an important question raised by Stukeley and Petrie: Did the builders have a unit of length, and if so, what was its value? Such a unit was undoubtedly used at Stonehenge. How are we to determine its value? It is not an easy problem. It is a matter of fractions of an inch, and the stones of the monument are not shaped regularly enough to give an adequate degree of precision. But after much groping and hesitation, fully realizing how conjectural such an estimate is, I have concluded that a cubit of 20.47 or 20.39 inches would apply rather well to the various dimensions of the monument. I am not claiming that it was actually used; I am simply saying that it may have been.*

Another question concerning the theoretical line of the Sarsen Circle: Which was decided beforehand, its diameter or its circumference? To a modern mind, that may seem a foolish question since the main thing that interests us in a circle is its diameter or radius. But consider the problem from the viewpoint of the builders on Salisbury Plain, thirteen or fourteen centuries before Christ. They were going to have to divide a circle into thirty equal parts, and they had no precision in-

*By analogy with the dagger carved on upright 53, it would be interesting to apply the cubit of 20.39 inches to various dimensions of the site at Mycenae. Unfortunately, I have been able to obtain very few really precise measurements. Two of them are for the "lion gate": 122.44 inches (10 feet 2.44 inches) high, 115.75 inches (9 feet 7.75 inches) wide at the base. The cubit of 20.39 inches can be applied as follows: $6 \times 20.39 = 122.34$, and $5\ 2/3 \times 20.30 = 115.54$. The total length of the corridor leading to "Agamemnon's tomb" is 245.04 inches (20 feet 5.04 inches), and $12 \times 20.39 = 244.68$. Other examples are said to be found not only at Mycenae but also at Orchomenus and other places. Since I have not been able to verify them, however, I will say no more about them.

It is not certain that another unit might not be equally well adapted to the measurements taken at those sites.

struments or trigonometric tables. Can we be certain that the circumference did not interest them?

We may also ask whether they really sought great precision in dividing their circle. A method of successive approximations might be considered if it were not for the lintels. Whatever their number may have been —28, 29, or 30—once they were joined, they had to form as regular a curve as possible. Since they were shaped before being put in place, their length and curvature had to be determined in advance. The curvature was relatively small, but it was still quite appreciable since its rise was 5 or 6 inches. A kind of pattern, with a length equal to one-thirtieth of the circumference, may have been used. In any case, there is nothing in the present state of the monument to indicate that the builders did not aim for a certain regularity. On the contrary, here are no obvious errors in the layout or division of the circle, and although it would be exaggerated to say that they achieved absolute precision, they did achieve a degree of accuracy that is amazing in view of their time, place, and materials.

But fixing the length of the circumference in advance implies knowledge of a value of pi. Personally, I see no reason to exclude the possibility of that knowledge among the people who built such an extraordinary monument. The ratio between the circumference and diameter of a circle, which we designate by the Greek letter pi, was known long before Stonehenge was built. The value attributed to it was 3.16, which, though not as accurate as its modern value, was adequate for construction work at that time.

If the builders decided that each division of the circle would be 6 cubits long, for example, the whole circumference measured 180 cubits. That length divided by 3.16 gives 57, to within less than a tenth of a unit. Fifty-seven cubits of 20.39 inches equals 96 feet 10 inches, which is the diameter of the Sarsen Circle to within a few inches. It is the diameter given by E. H. Stone. If we take the cubit of 20.47 inches, we obtain a diameter of 97 feet 3 inches, which is very close to the one given by Petrie (97 feet 4 inches) and accepted by Atkinson. And if the length of the circumference was taken not as 180 cubits but as 360 ancient feet (half cubits), the number would correspond to the sexagesimal division of the circle into degrees. That division was known in the ancient world, notably by the Egyptians, who used a foot with a value of 10.2 modern inches. The builders could then have laid out a circle with a radius of 28½ cubits, or 57 ancient feet.

Returning to Figure 27, let us divide the distance H′H into two equal parts. We now have point A, which corresponds to the middle of the space between uprights 1 and 30 in the Sarsen Circle. From that point, let us measure a distance of 28½ cubits, or 57 ancient feet. We obtain the center O of the monument. That center will always be easy to find again since $H'O + OA = AH$ and $HO/H'O = 1.6$, approximately.* The builders could then lay out the circle, but how did they divide it into thirty equal parts?

The following procedure, which I described with regard to the circle of the Aubrey Holes, may have been used. Small stakes could have been placed all around the circle, close enough together to occupy the whole curve. A thong with a length of 6 cubits, or 12 ancient feet, applied successively to the stakes, would give the divisions of the circle. Other possible procedures can be imagined, of course. I will give one in an appendix.

When the circle had been divided into thirty equal parts, the builders could begin digging the holes for the uprights. These holes had to be dug with great care. When the uprights had been erected, their inner surfaces had to be in the same vertical plane, 5 feet below the ground or 13 feet above it. In other words, the contour of the circle had to be very nearly the same at a depth of 5 feet underground as at the surface and

*In the calculations I have indicated, any differences that may exist are a matter of only a few inches. They come from the fact that we calculate with the decimal system, and the Stonehenge builders did not. It was more difficult for them to handle decimal numbers.

at the height of the lintels. Although some correction was possible, the error in digging the foundation holes had to be very small. The holes were of different depths because the uprights all had to have the same height above ground, but their total lengths were different.

The process of erecting them was not particularly difficult. Inclined planes leading down to the bottom of the holes brought them into an oblique position.* The effort required to pull them erect with ropes was then greatly diminished, especially if the ropes passed over crossbeams before reaching the men who pulled on them. Since the ends of some uprights were rather pointed, beams must have been held against their sides to keep them from pivoting. Logs placed against the inside of the hole lessened the risk of damage when the upright rubbed against it.

The most important thing was to have the holes accurately placed around the circle. The inclined planes were outside the circle since the stones were brought from that direction. During the restoration work of 1958, however, it was discovered that the inclined plane used for erecting upright 21 was inside the circle. The reason for this is not known. The ramp of the neighboring restored upright, number 22, is on the outside.

I believe the cause of that anomaly is related to construction of the trilithons. Erection of upright 21 may have been delayed to allow the stones of the trilithons to be brought in. If we look at Figure 7, we see that upright 21 could not have been erected by pulling on it from inside the monument when trilithon 57–58 was in place because upright 58 would have interfered with the operation. But there was plenty of space outside the circle. Since the same would also have been true of

*Not all the holes had such a ramp. Sarsen upright 6 and the uprights of trilithon 57–58 had none. They must have been short stones whose foundations were shallower than the others. I cannot imagine how they were erected. The difficulties to be overcome must have been enormous. I regard the operation as an extraordinary feat.

upright 22, it must have been erected before the trilithon was in place.

Many British authors believe that the trilithons were built before the Sarsen Circle. They base their opinion on the size of the uprights, especially their thickness, which is greater than that of the uprights in the circle. They forget that the space between stones 11 and 12 was about 5½ feet, whereas the greatest thickness of a trilithon upright, probably that of number 54, was a little less than 5 feet. The uprights had to be moved on edge, of course, but that was not impossible. Furthermore, erection of stone 11, like that of 21, may have been delayed until all the trilithon uprights had been brought in. These are the smallest and most irregularly placed stones in the circle. Finally, as we will see, the builders encountered great difficulties in erecting upright 56, and those difficulties would not have existed without the Sarsen Circle.

The main reason that makes me believe that the Sarsen Circle was built before the trilithons is that if the trilithons had been built first, they would have made it impossible to lay out the circle again or correct it if necessary. If for any reason the stakes marking the circle had disappeared, the possibility of an accurate layout would have been greatly diminished. I do not know in what sequence the work was actually done, but I am certain that if I had to build an identical monument, I would begin by erecting the stones of the outer circle.

In the construction of Stonehenge, the hardest, longest, and most dangerous work must surely have been putting the lintels of the Sarsen Circle in place. How did the builders manage to perch 6-ton stones at such a height and fit them together so well?

If their method of assembly had been limited to one kind of joint—either mortises and tenons, as in the trilithons, or V-shaped joints—their tasks would have been easier, but with both at once it was very complicated. Each lintel had to be somehow raised above its two uprights and then lowered onto them, so that their tenons would fit into its mortises. And at the same time the tongue of its V-shaped joint had to fit into the groove of the lintel next to it. Or the lintels may first have been joined end to end, above the uprights, and then lowered onto them. If the reader will look at Figure 8, he will understand what I mean.

The first job was obviously to raise the lintels above the uprights. We do not know how that was done. It is relatively easy to imagine how the stones were transported since the possible means were limited; it is harder to imagine how such a remarkable feat as raising the lintels was accomplished.

The first means that comes to mind is an inclined plane made of earth. Once the uprights had been erected, a ramp could have been built all the way to their tops. This is the method suggested by E. H. Stone. It would have required a considerable amount of work, but it could have been done. If, as I believe, the whole inside of the Sarsen Circle was filled in, with an extension of about 20 feet beyond it, the total volume of earth was about 500,000 cubic feet, 600,000 at the most. It was not an impossible task. Two thousand men could have done it in twenty days, including the tamping. For the people who had brought the stones from the Marlborough Downs, it was scarcely a problem at all. In any case, it was the simplest and most practical method. It must have been used for putting the slabs of dolmens in place, and many believe it was also used in building the Egyptian pyramids.

It has been objected that there is now no trace of such an earthwork, but why should there be? There is no trace of a similar earthwork around most dolmens, either. The operation does not seem to have affected the circular ditch and bank. Perhaps the builders wanted to respect the henge monument even though they had not taken its layout into account. Since a temple was built in the middle of it, the site had a certain importance. Be that as it may, the necessary 600,000 cubic feet of earth could have been obtained by removing a 4-inch layer from an area of 42 acres. I see no reason to believe that this was unfeasible.

Systems using wood have been proposed, notably

by R. H. Cunnington in his book *Stonehenge and Its Date*. His method is hard to describe in detail, but it consists essentially in lifting the stones onto successive wooden platforms. Although it is very ingenious, it has the disadvantages of requiring a great amount of timberwork, being very long and, especially, not giving the workers enough freedom to maneuver. They would have had to lift 6-ton stones to a height of 13 feet, using only levers. It is prudent not to accept this hypothesis unless a more plausible version of it can be devised.

But if the workers had a solid earth platform at the height of the uprights, it was much easier for them to lift the lintels, fit them in place, check their level and curvature, and make corrections if necessary. It was as if they were working on the ground.

If a certain regularity was sought in the Sarsen Circle, it was mainly at the level of the lintels because there is only an approximate regularity at the bases of the uprights. And the lintels of the trilithons also had to be put in place. During the restoration work of 1958, the lintel of trilithon 57–58 was lifted above the uprights by a 60-ton crane. Even with that powerful machine, fitting the lintel was not an easy operation. What would it have been like with wooden planking around and above 40-ton monoliths sunk less than 4 feet into the ground? Another important advantage of filling in the whole Sarsen Circle is that the plan of the entire sarsen structure could have been laid out again with stakes on top of that earthen mountain. The circle would, of course, have been filled in after the uprights of the trilithons had been erected.

I have already said that the upper surfaces of the lintels were horizontal with a remarkable degree of accuracy. How was that accuracy achieved? Probably by means of one of the oldest known instruments: a piece of wood in the shape of a right-angled triangle, with a plumb line hanging from the vertex of the right angle. The hypotenuse is placed on the surface to be checked. When the plumb line hangs down at the middle of the hypotenuse, the surface is horizontal. This instrument was known to the Egyptians at the time when the pyramids were built. The Stonehenge builders may also have used a container filled with water as a kind of spirit level, but the triangle with a plumb line would have been more practical.

Whatever instrument was used, corrections must not have been easy. An initial adjustment was made when the uprights were erected: As we have seen, they do not all sink into the ground to the same depth. The final correction may have been made by grinding down the upper surfaces of the lintels. The earthen platform around the uprights would have made all this work much easier.

The positioning of the great sarsen trilithons, the most impressive feature of the monument, poses a difficult problem in study of the plan of Stonehenge. They were certainly not placed at random, or even in an approximate way. Since their vertical dimensions appear to have been carefully planned, the same was undoubtedly true of their positioning in the structure.

The location of the central trilithon presents no difficulty. It stood astride the Axis, and its center was 25 feet 6 inches from the center of the monument, a distance equal to its total height. It also seems that if an arc of a circle with a radius of 25 feet 6 inches is drawn from the center of the monument, it passes through the centers of the two neighboring trilithons, 53–54 and 57–58. In Figure 28 I have marked the centers of these three trilithons as d, e, and c. I say "it seems" because verification at the site is very difficult. My conclusion is based on the plan shown in Figure 28. If it is correct, we can see how the positioning of trilithons 53–54 and 57–58 would have been facilitated.

The positioning of trilithons 51–52 and 59–60 may also have been facilitated on the basis of the following considerations. Line cd cuts line H'H at point f, and line ab, joining the centers of the two trilithons, cuts it at point g. The length of line fg is 25 feet 6 inches, and that of ab is 48 feet 6 inches, which is the radius of the Sarsen Circle.

But the centers of the trilithons were not sufficient

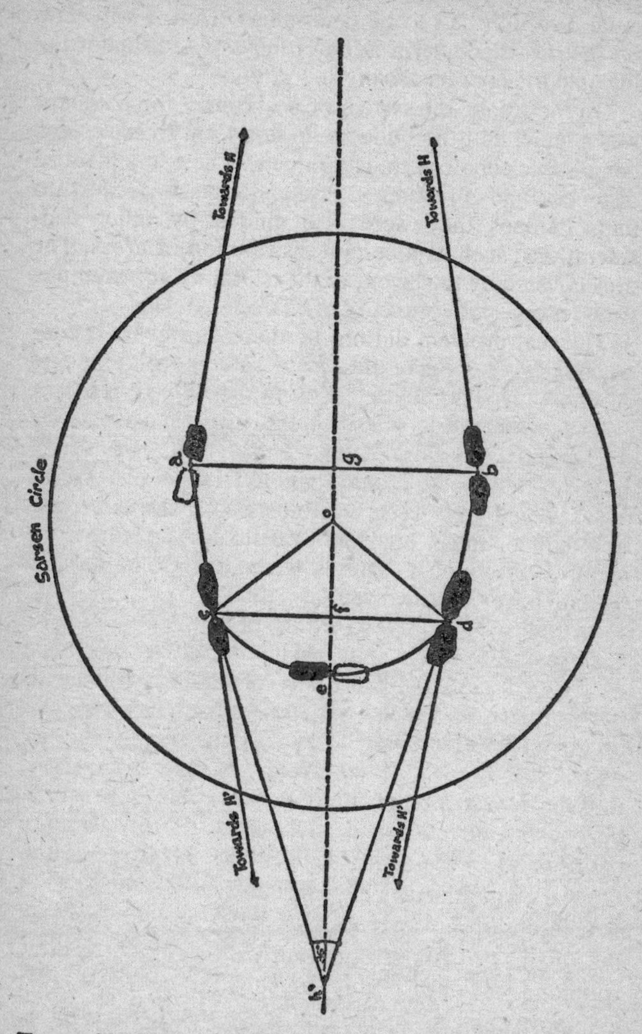

FIGURE 28—How the positions of the trilithons may have been laid out.

for positioning them. With four of them, their longitudinal direction had to be determined. Here I will state no theories since verification is impossible without being able to perch on top of the trilithons.

On the whole, the system of positioning the trilithons was simple, and the builders do not seem to have used complex calculations to determine it. They only planned distances and directions, or angles that were easy to find. Perhaps they were also guided by other considerations, such as a certain distribution of areas. The area covered by the layout of the trilithons, for example, is about one-sixth of that of the Sarsen Circle.

The real problem did not lie there, however. It consisted in always being able to lay out the plan on the ground, no matter what stage the work had reached. I have already discussed the difficulty of maintaining the layout in a reduced area. Finally, there was verification of the location and orientation of the trilithons, which would have been difficult without a system outside the monument, making it possible to find the main features of the plan. This is where the Four Stations seem to have been involved.

Once the location and orientation of the trilithons had been determined, there was no difficulty in digging the holes and ramps. I do not know on which side the ramps were dug, that is, from which direction the uprights were brought to be erected. British authors say that the ramps for the trilithons were dug in the center-outward direction and in the opposite direction for the uprights of the Sarsen Circle. That seems natural if the work was done as I have assumed.

One curious case is worth considering. It involves the ramp used for erecting upright 56 of the central trilithon, the longest and probably the heaviest stone in the monument. In the course of the 1958 restoration work, when preparations were being made for reerecting trilithon 57–58, the workers discovered a kind of trench that became increasingly deeper as it approached the foot of upright 56. It had been dug into the chalk and later filled in. It was undoubtedly the ramp that had been used for erecting the upright.

It is strange that this ramp was not detected during Gowland's re-erection work in 1901. He thought that he recognized the inclined plane, coming from inside, and that bluestone 68 had been erected in the earth with which the trench was filled in. He had presumably encountered traces of earlier excavations, perhaps those of the Duke of Buckingham.

But the direction of the trench recognized in 1958 is perpendicular to the axis of the monument. It is shown in broken lines and marked A in Figure 7. It seems to indicate two possibilities: Either the stone was slid along the ramp on its wide side and then pivoted 90 degrees after it was standing, or it was slid on edge and erected in the same position. In either case the operation was risky if not dangerous, and the builders must have had a serious reason for proceeding in that way. The work was obviously carried out under masterful guidance. What modern engineer would dare to attempt such an operation with the means available at that time?

Placing the Bluestone Horseshoe inside the horseshoe formed by the trilithons presented no difficulty. Its circular part had a diameter of 35 feet 8 inches and contained eleven stones; it therefore had ten intervals if we assume a stone on the Axis. A certain symmetry was observed, but on the whole the distribution is far from being as precise as in the sarsen structure.

Finally, there was the Bluestone Circle. It undoubtedly could not have been laid out completely on the ground. This resulted in features I have already mentioned: pairs of stones at opposite ends of a single diameter and lines of sight to the center. The best-preserved group is near the entrance, that is, in the part of the monument that can be seen best from the center. I have also mentioned that, judging from the results of work done at Stonehenge in the past fifty years, many bluestones other than those now visible once stood in the circle, but I do not believe the whole circle has yet been explored, so it is better to wait for the results of future research before forming a final opinion.

There is nothing particular to report about the location of the Altar Stone except that the distance from its center to that of the monument seems to have been 10 feet 2 inches, which is 6 cubits or 12 ancient feet. It does not occupy an outstanding place in the plan of the structure. The Axis presumably divided it into two equal parts. Its present location and its obliquity in relation to the Axis seem to have resulted from the fall of upright 55 and the forward motion of one of its fragments.

To conclude the discussion of the construction of Stonehenge, I will point out one more singular detail: As soon as stone 67 had been erected in the Bluestone Horseshoe, the geometrical center of the monument could no longer be found except by trial and error. Stone 67 stood on line H'H and made it impossible to locate that important point precisely. To the best of my knowledge, nothing has yet been found at the center, not even a post hole, to show that its position was indicated at least once by a physical marker. Nor are there, within the temple itself, any alignments that intersect at that point, judging from the present state of the ruins and the plan of the structure. It almost seems, in fact, that the builders wanted it to be lost, but the mathematical center may never have existed on the ground: It may have been above it, at the level of the lintels. It is easy to understand why such a skilled observer as Petrie found three or four different centers.

Solar Observations*

We here approach the most debated and debatable problem but also the most fascinating. How was sunrise at the summer solstice observed through the monument? Did the monument permit other observations of

*Before reading this section, I advise the reader to review those devoted to the Heel Stone (Part One) and Lockyer's work (Part Two).

the same kind? Let us note the importance of these questions. On their answers depend the ideas we can form about the purpose of Stonehenge, the date of its construction, and the astronomical knowledge of its builders. If it was designed to mark midsummer sunrise at the time when it was built, or similar phenomena, enduring indications of that intention still remain, and how valuable they will be if we can find them!

As I have said, the place of the observer had to be permanently fixed. It would have been enough to require him to sight along two markers on line H'H. One of them may have been a stone near H'; the other may have been the left side of the Heel Stone, point H.

Let us see how that line crossed the monument. Since it was an axis of symmetry, it passed through the centers of the following intervals (Figure 29):

1. Uprights 15 and 16 in the Sarsen Circle.
2. Uprights 55 and 56 of the central trilithon.
3. Stones 31 and 49 in the Bluestone Circle.
4. Uprights 1 and 30 in the Sarsen Circle.
5. The Slaughter Stone and its companion.

We will also assume that it crossed stone 67 in the horseshoe, divided the Altar Stone in two, touched the left side of the Heel Stone, and extended toward the point on the horizon at which the sun rose at the summer solstice.

Let us examine each of those points in turn. First, the interval between uprights 15 and 16 in the Sarsen Circle. Only 16 is still standing, 15 being represented by a fragment on the ground. We do not know what the distance between them was when they were both standing, but there is no reason to suppose that it was much greater or smaller than average. That the Axis passed 2 feet 7 inches to the right of upright 16 would seem to indicate that the space was 5 feet 2 inches, or 1 foot 8 inches more than the others. Such a difference would be noticeable if the presumed location of upright 15 were excavated, but an abnormal interval would not be

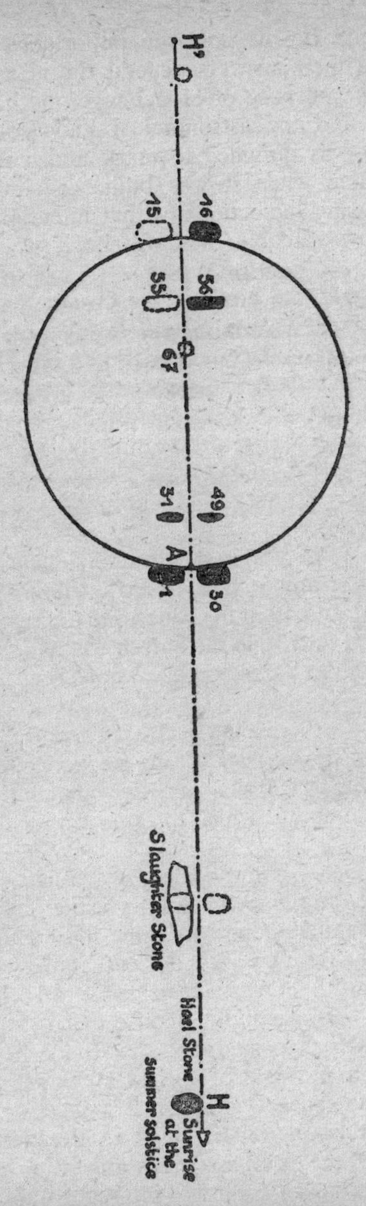

FIGURE 29—The sighting system.

very important. Let us simply note that line H'H passed 1 foot 10 inches to the right of upright 16. That distance corresponds to the average interval of the other uprights.

Let us consider the position of the Great Trilithon. It is the only important part of the monument that has a geometric relation to the Axis since it is perpendicular to it.* That is why it has always been thought to be related to solar observation in some way. In view of its position, that seems obvious. If it were not true, the whole structure would not be related to such observations. But here again an element is missing. Only one of the two uprights is still standing, so the distance between them cannot be measured, which is fortunate for those who maintain that it is impossible to determine whether or not the structure was oriented toward midsummer sunrise. That is a hasty judgment, in my opinion.

The exact distance between the two uprights will probably never be known, but there are still enough remaining elements to give a very close estimate of it. The Axis passes 1 foot 6 inches to the right of upright 56, which would seem to indicate an interval of 3 feet. E. H. Stone tried to demonstrate this with calculations on the basis of the positions of the mortises and tenons. But that interval would be too great. The width of upright 56 is 6 feet 11 inches, and that of upright 55 is 7 feet 5 inches. If we add Stone's interval of 3 feet, we have a total width of 17 feet 4 inches for the trilithon. But the lintel, whose length should be equal to that distance, is actually only 15 feet 3 inches long.*

The present average distance between the two uprights is 1 foot 1 inch. If it was originally 3 feet, up-

*The same may have been true of the Altar Stone, but it probably did not stand upright.

*In his book, Stone himself gives a drawing of the restored trilithon with the following dimensions: length of the lintel: 16 feet; width of each upright: 7 feet 6 inches.
That leaves only one foot for the interval. Even if we add a few inches to allow for entasis, we are still far from 3 feet.

right 55 moved nearly 2 feet sideways when it fell. That is unlikely for a stone that weighs 45 tons and therefore has great inertia. It now forms an angle of 6 or 7 degrees with the Axis, caused by the fall of the lintel, which tended to shear off the tenon. If the distance between the two uprights had originally been 3 feet, that angle would have been much greater, at least 15 or 20 degrees.

Judging from the present positions of the uprights, their interval must not have been very different from what it is now: 1 foot 1 inch. This opinion is supported by an experiment reproducing the fall of the lintel and upright 55 with a model of the trilithon. The interval was estimated at 1 foot 1 inch by Petrie and at 2 feet by Lockyer, who was obviously influenced by the Axis. The question may some day be settled by excavations locating the hole in which upright 55 stood.

Line H'H passes a little less than 8 inches to the right of upright 56. After marking the center of the monument, it crosses the centers of the spaces between stones 49 and 31 in the Bluestone Circle and uprights 1 and 30 in the Sarsen Circle. Before reaching point H, it passes about a foot and a half to the left of the Slaughter Stone.

As we have seen, that stone had a companion whose position has been rediscovered. Unfortunately, I have not been able even to estimate the distance between the holes of the two stones. If the Slaughter Stone and its companion formed a marker on the line of sight, they must have been more than 3 feet apart. If they were placed symmetrically in relation to line H'H, that distance would not be impossible since the line passes about a foot and a half from the Slaughter Stone. The Axis itself must not be more than 2 feet from it. But if we look at the plans published by Newall or Atkinson, the distance is 4 feet 11 inches or 6 feet 7 inches. To conclude, then, I will say that if the two stones were symmetrical in relation to line H'H, their interval was a little more than 3 feet, and if they were not, that fact was rather abnormal.

The line of sight ended at point H, the left side of

the Heel Stone. This point may occasionally have been marked with a stake. Line H'H does not differ greatly from Petrie's Axis. The difference is so slight, in fact—14 minutes, which amounts to less than 10 inches at point H—that they can be regarded as identical. The slightest revision or correction of the calculations would probably bring them even closer together. When solar observations are made with rudimentary means, the length of the line of sight is an important factor. In the case of line H'H, it was about 400 feet, which was enough to give good accuracy.

The above considerations are rather arid, and I apologize to the reader for it, but I wanted to make my study as thorough as possible. To a large extent, the problems raised by Stonehenge turn on such questions of inches. We cannot ignore them if we want to understand not only past controversies but also, most likely, those that will take place in the future.

What was the position of the sun at the time of observation? Three possibilities can reasonably be considered:

1. The upper edge of the sun just emerging above the horizon.
2. Its center on the horizon.
3. Its lower edge tangent to the horizon.

R. H. Stone seriously concerned himself with that question and concluded that the first position had to be the one that was used. I do not know if he tried the experiment for himself, or if most of those who now discuss the matter have done so. Such questions seem so simple that people often believe they can be settled by putting a few words on paper. Faithful to my method, I have tried to situate the appearance of the first ray of light from the sun at Stonehenge, and I have learned how hard it is to do. What is seen is often not a point but a short, blazing streak whose center is elusive. By the time the position of a marker can be corrected, the spot of light has become larger and moved to the right. In a few seconds the sun has passed through a minute of angle, and it is almost too late. On the basis of my experiments, using only direct observation with the means available at the time when Stonehenge was built, I believe that the appearance of the sun's upper edge on the horizon was too fleeting to give good accuracy. At most, it may have been used as a preliminary sign.

The second position, with half the sun above the horizon, offers better possibilities. The sun's apparent diameter can be determined even with rudimentary means. Two pairs of stakes, one placed 164 feet away from the observer with an interval of 18 inches, the other 328 feet away with an interval of 38 inches, will frame the sun when it is halfway above the horizon, and there is time to see that this condition has been fulfilled. This was the method that the Incan priests used for determining the solstices, judging from what was reported by Betanzos and Garcilaso de la Vega. In his *Roman Questions,* Plutarch wrote, "Mathematicians fixed the limit between day and night when the center of the sun was on the circle of the horizon." It is the most logical method and the one least subject to ambiguity.

I have situated the observation point—or at least the most important one, the one that made it possible to fix the summer solstice with the greatest accuracy—at H′. The gaze of an observer standing or sitting at that place probably passed over stone 67. But if we imagine an observer there on a morning corresponding to our June 21, it becomes apparent that he must not have seen much except the dark mass of the uprights and lintels against the background of a pink and red sky.

Only a thin, vertical streak of light came through the space between the uprights of the Great Trilithon. That was enough. Soon a bright spot appeared at the edge of the left upright, number 56. The glowing disk of the sun gradually rose till it was precisely framed between the two uprights. Its center was on the horizon.

It had reached the end of its northward motion. This was the longest day of the year.

The phenomenon had been foreseen six or seven days in advance, when the spot of light appeared at the edge of upright 55. The first appearance of the sun moved across the narrow space between the two uprights. At the same time, an increasingly large part of it was seen above the horizon until half of it was in the interval. The same process then took place in reverse, so that some part of the sun could be seen between the uprights of the Great Trilithon for about two weeks. To see this, the observer had to be at point H′ and nowhere else.

Many other things could be ascertained if we were certain of the position of upright 55. But there is one element that will probably always be in doubt: the height at which the observer placed himself. He may have been exactly at point H′, on top of the bank, but he may also have been behind or in front of it. If so, he was in a lower position. Furthermore, we do not know the original height of the bank. It is generally estimated at about 6 feet, but it may have been lower at H′. If it was too high, the observer stood farther down, in the direction of the monument. In any case, observation was conditioned by center stone 67 in the Bluestone Horseshoe since the observer's gaze had to pass above it. If that stone were re-erected, the doubt would be less great.

The Great Trilithon is 138 feet away from H′. At that distance, the apparent diameter of the sun is 15 inches. It is 2 feet at the space between stones 1 and 30 in the Sarsen Circle, exactly halfway between the Great Trilithon and H′. Finally, it is 3 feet at the Slaughter Stone, and this is twice the distance between that stone and line H′H. Let us examine the part that the Slaughter Stone may have played in the sighting system. (See Figures 29 and 30.)

One important fact, already pointed out by Cunnington and Barclay, must be noted at the outset: If the Slaughter Stone originally stood upright, it blocked out

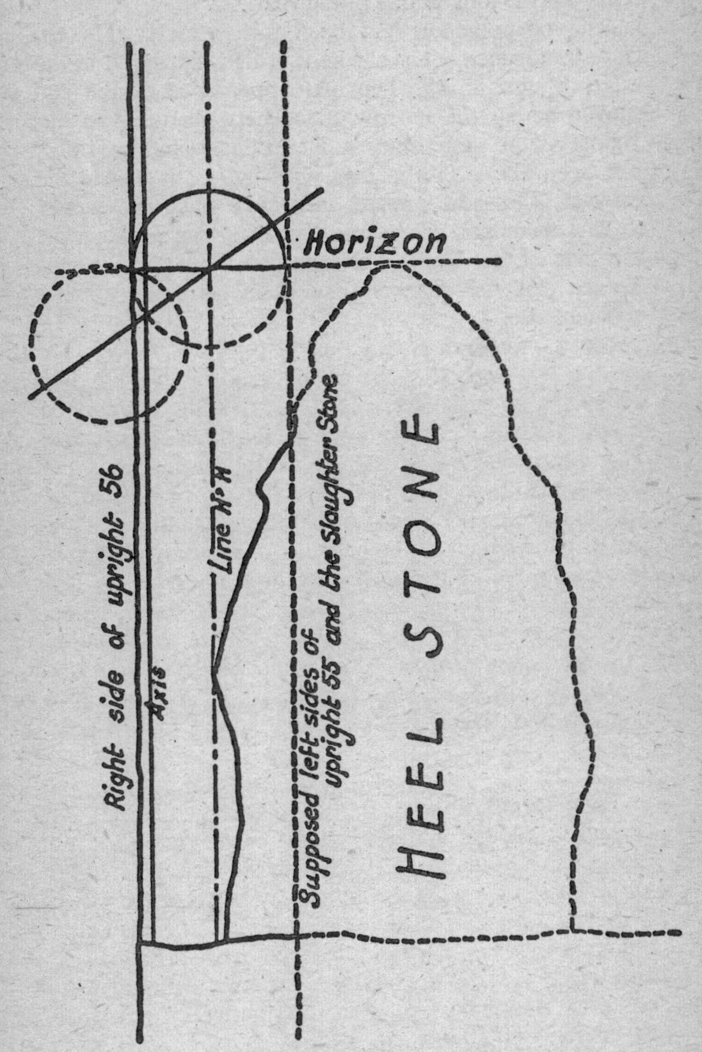
Horizon
Right side of upright 56
Axis
Supposed left sides of upright 55 and the Slaughter Stone
HEEL STONE

FIGURE 30

more than half of the Heel Stone from the center of the monument. (And therefore, if it were re-erected, it would be a cause of disappointment to the thousands of visitors on the morning of June 21.) This fact would seem to indicate that the top of the Heel Stone played no part in solar observations. In Figure 29 we see that if the Slaughter Stone were standing, it would mark the line of sight, so that it and upright 56 would be enough to frame half of the sun from the viewpoint of an observer at H′. We may always assume, of course, that a vertical stake was planted at point H, next to the Heel Stone.

The sighting system may have been set up as follows: the interval between the uprights of the Great Trilithon, and then the interval between the Slaughter Stone and its companion. Those two spaces of 15 inches and 3 feet exactly correspond to the apparent diameter of the sun as seen from H′. I scarcely dare to think that this was actually the system used, however, because Stonehenge would then have been the most precise solar observatory in the ancient world since it would have made it possible to determine the summer solstice to within one day. I know of nothing equivalent.

Let us now consider whether other noteworthy directions could be observed in the monument. I do not intend to look for any within the structure itself. With such a dense concentration of stones in a limited area, anyone can find practically any direction he wants. I will therefore disregard the Sarsen Circle and everything inside it, with one exception, which I will discuss later.

I will remind the reader that the holes marked F, G, and K in Figure 4 have been recognized as having once served to hold standing stones. They are approximately on the circle of the Four Stations. Here, in my opinion, are the directions worth mentioning: (See Figure 31.)

1. Point H′ to station 93 indicates the north-south direction, and the same is true of the line from station 91 to point F.
2. Point H′ to point K shows the east-west direction

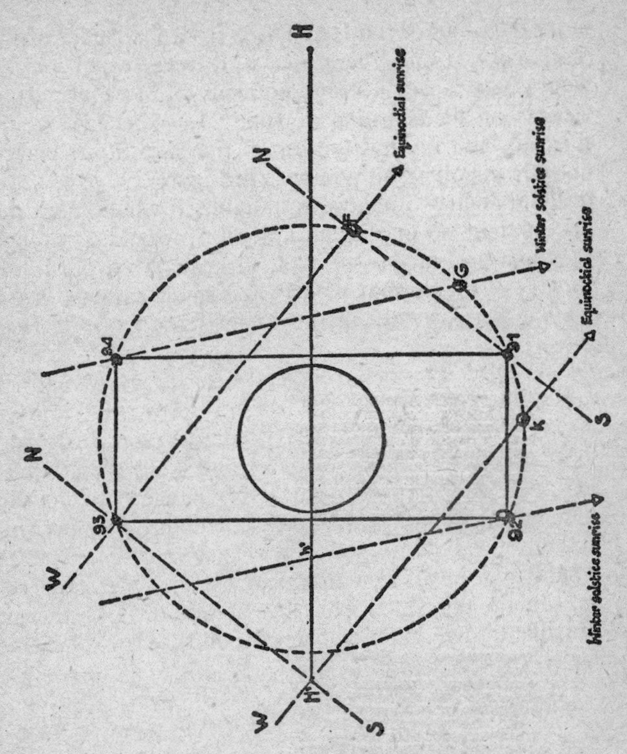

FIGURE 31—How outstanding sunrises may have been inscribed in the circle of the Four Stations.

and, consequently, sunrise at the equinoxes. The same is true of the line between station 93 and point F.

3. Station 94 to point G marks sunrise at the winter solstice.

I will also point out that lines 92–91 and 93–94 are in the direction of sunrise at the summer solstice. The monument does not interfere with these lines since they are outside it. I am not, of course, saying that they were used; I am simply saying that such observations were possible.

There is a rather curious phenomenon that can be observed inside the monument by anyone who is there a little before apparent noon. It is strange that no one has reported it before. If the sun is not veiled by clouds, it casts a streak of light on the ground inside the monument, through the space between the uprights of trilithon 53–54. As the sun continues its motion, the streak dwindles to a fine line and finally disappears. At that moment the sun is over the meridian of Stonehenge. It is apparent noon, and the line has precisely marked the north-south direction. (See Figure 32.) The line

FIGURE 32

does not pass through the center. I give this detail for whatever it may be worth.

To me, the real history of Stonehenge ended when the sun no longer remained chained to its stone pillars. It stayed there for long centuries, but eventually there came a time when half of its disk was no longer exactly framed between the uprights of the Great Trilithon. That ran counter to an ancient tradition. The first rays of the sun still appeared between the two giant stones, but the longest day of the year became more and more difficult to determine. Finally, only a quarter of the disk showed between the two uprights. The sun god was forsaking his worshipers, and that withdrawal from a frame that had seemed established for all eternity appeared to be ineluctable. If some sort of disaster—an epidemic, an invasion, a famine—then struck the tribes on Salisbury Plain, it must have been enough to make them abandon the temple.

Then came other peoples, other beliefs . . .

Conclusion

It is now possible to measure the distance that has been traveled since the already remote time when Inigo Jones, John Aubrey, and William Stukeley made their investigations. We have seen the groping, errors, and patient work involved in the process of gradually lifting the veil that covered Stonehenge. At first sight, it seems that we are now able to answer the great questions: Why? When? How? By whom?

Why was Stonehenge built? I have assumed without discussion that it was meant to be a solar temple. And that is the general opinion, although there are those who say that we actually know nothing about the purpose of the monument and that a scientific mind should not go beyond what has been proved. There are arguments in favor of such an attitude, but if all we are entitled to say about Stonehenge is that it is a collection of stones shaped and arranged in certain ways on Salisbury Plain, we may as well turn away from those stones and take an interest in something else.

I do not have the same feeling about the worship that may have been celebrated in the temple or the symbolism of the figures formed by the uprights. I have not ventured into that area because I have no knowledge of such subjects. Everyone is free to form his own judgment on them. It would be ridiculous to estimate the diameter of the Sarsen Circle according to one's personal taste, but it is perfectly legitimate to imagine priests officiating on the Altar Stone and a crowd of worshipers gathered around the peristyle. One may also think that the nineteen bluestones of the horseshoe represent the Metonic cycle, that the uprights of the Sarsen Circle symbolize the thirty days of a month, or other things in the same vein. They are all permissible because one quality of such a monument is that it makes the imagination wander around it.

When was it built? In either the fourteenth or fifteenth century B.C., but precision is not very important here. Dating Stonehenge to within a century or two is sufficient to place it in a context. It was built before the Celts and after the Neolithic populations, that is, at a time when copper and bronze were known but not iron.

How was it built? Work done in this century has brought to light the plan followed by the builders. Archaeologists have found the distant origin of the stones and examined nearly all possible methods of erecting the uprights and putting their lintels in place. Those matters have been given explanations that, if not certain, are at least reasonable, and it is unlikely that they will be drastically altered by future research.

Who were the builders of Stonehenge? Modern archaeology has retraced the series of populations that occupied Wiltshire after the Neolithic dawn: the peoples of Windmill Hill, the megaliths, the Secondary Neolithic and the Beakers, and finally the Wessex Culture. The various stages of Stonehenge can be attributed to those peoples. The sarsen structure, in particular, seems to be the work of those who made the rich round barrows in the environs.

We are thus very close to giving convincing answers to the main questions. Yet a kind of uneasiness still remains. The mind is not entirely satisfied. The answers found were, so to speak, expected of modern science. They are not surprising, and the same could have been done with any other prehistoric monument. It is as if we were told nothing about the Eiffel Tower except that it was built in about 1890, of iron from the Briey

Basin, by workers from Les Batignolles and Pantin, in order to give a panoramic view of Paris. There would be nothing false in that, but who would be satisfied with it?

The unique character of Stonehenge shows that it is the work of a single man. And that man was foreign to Salisbury Plain. That is the only reasonable conclusion I can reach. It is nearly certain that the people of the Wessex Culture built the monument, but none of them conceived its plan. They simply supplied the labor. Between their civilization and that represented by the sarsen structure, there is at least a thousand years of cultural progress. And I am convinced that Stonehenge has not yet revealed everything. To say that its design grew out of the local culture would be to say that pure science, at that time and place, had advanced to a stage comparable to its level in Egypt and Chaldea. That is not conceivable since many centuries had to pass before monuments representing such an advanced stage of civilization appeared in Western Europe.

Where did that brilliant architect come from? The Aegean dagger carved on one of the trilithons probably tells us the direction in which we should look. Not that he carved it himself—he no doubt had better things to do—but we know from Pausanias that there was a group of thirty stones at Pherae, in Thessaly, beside a statue of Hermes, the god of commerce. Those stones were worshiped as gods. We also know that in archaic Greece the shapes given to sacred stones were of two types: the cone and the parallelogram, the latter being consecrated to Hermes. These are the two aspects of the shaped stones we see at Stonehenge; the bluestones of the horseshoe are rather conical.

The great magician probably came from one of the countries around the eastern part of the Mediterranean. Only there could one have learned enough geometry, architecture, and astronomy to design such a monument. It does not matter whether that country was Argolis, Crete, Egypt, Phoenicia, or some other; the main point is that the architect came from a country with a civilization that had long been highly developed.

Perhaps he was one of the itinerant philosophers so numerous in ancient times. How did that precursor of men like Thales and Pythagoras reach the great northern island? Probably by the same route as the amber and tin traders. It is a mistake to judge the geographical knowledge of the ancients only on the basis of classical writers. Centuries before Strabo, and even before Herodotus, a Tyrian sea captain knew much more than they about the coasts of the Atlantic. The "Greek miracle" was not manifested in geography.

There is nothing surprising about the fact that a man with an encyclopedic mind reached Great Britain at that time since there were commercial relations between his country and Western Europe. Furthermore, he must have had no difficulty in persuading the people of Wiltshire to build a magnificent circular temple dedicated to the sun god. They had long been accustomed to carrying out enormous collective tasks, represented by the megalithic monuments. They may even have asked for his help since the influence of those who know is sometimes very great.

It has been said that Stonehenge was by far the most impressive prehistoric monument north of the pyramids. That phrase haunted me a long time and still haunts me as I bring this book to a close. I have never thought of drawing any kind of parallel between two such different monuments, but it has always seemed to me that, like the Egyptian engineers, the designer of Stonehenge included certain scientific knowledge in his work. I have said nothing about that idea in this book because it is purely speculative.

It may seem to be merely coincidental that ten times the perimeter of the Sarsen Circle equals the perimeter of the Great Pyramid or that thirty times its height equals the height of that same pyramid. It is a matter of personal preference. Here is another case, probably also fortuitous: If the circumference of the Sarsen Circle is multiplied by the product of $100 \times 12 \times 360$, the result is 131, 645, 185 feet, or 24,933 miles, which is very close to the earth's circumference. This also means that the circumference of the Sarsen Circle is equal to half a minute of arc on a meridian of the earth. Other coincidences of the same kind could probably be pointed out, but what does that mean? That Apollo's arrow, on which the magician Abaris is said to have traveled over the earth, was included in the temple in a veiled form? That Eratosthenes' calculation of the earth's circumference had actually been performed fifteen or sixteen centuries earlier? What do we know about such things? What will tomorrow's archaeology tell us?

Myths and legends have hidden meanings. We are becoming increasingly aware that they are like cryptograms waiting to be decoded. In spite of everything, they remain a fragile link between us and a remote past. That is why the memory of the brilliant master builder of Stonehenge has not entirely faded away. He still lives in the legendary figure of King Arthur's counselor, and Stonehenge is still the Dance of the Giants, brought to Salisbury Plain from a faraway land by Merlin the Enchanter.

APPENDICES

Appendix 1

The Division of the Sarsen Circle into Thirty Equal Parts

If the builders knew how to inscribe regular polygons in a circle, they had geometrical means at their disposal and were not forced to rely on trial-and-error methods.

Let us say, for example, that xy is the side of a pentagon inscribed in a circle with its center at O (Figure 33). Angle xoy is 72 degrees. If, on radius

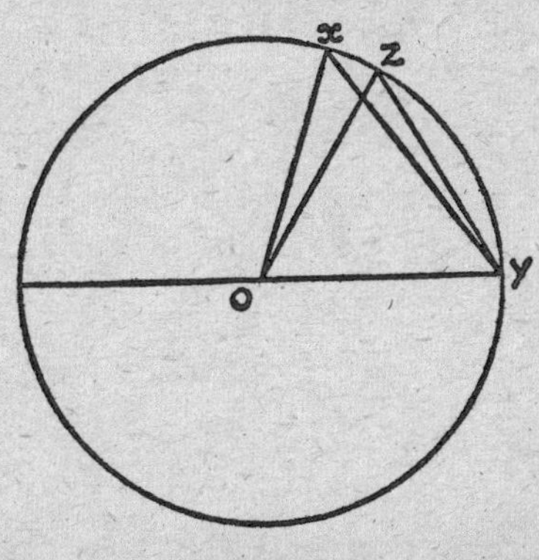

FIGURE 33

oy, we draw an equilateral triangle, or if (which comes to the same thing) we inscribe a hexagon with a side zy, angle zoy will be 60 degrees.

The difference between the two angles, that is, angle xoz, is 12 degrees, corresponding to one-thirtieth of the circumference.

Since 57 ancient feet is the length of the radius of the circle, the length of the side of the pentagon is 67 ancient feet.

$\frac{67}{57} = 1.175$, or $\frac{57}{2}\sqrt{10 - 2\sqrt{5}}$, which is the side of the pentagon to within two one-thousandths.

The coincidence is remarkable, and I will add that the pentagon and the hexagon were known to the Babylonians and Egyptians centuries before the construction of Stonehenge.

Appendix 2

The Rectangle of the Four Stations

This figure, as I have said, could have been used to locate the axis and center of the temple. It seems to me that other elements were included in it, notably astronomical data distinctive of the location of Stonehenge.

Let us consider rectangle ABCD, formed by the Four Stations (Figure 34). The ratio of the sides of this figure is 12 to 5, since their lengths are 262.25 and 108.67 feet, and $262.25 \div 108.67 = 2.4 = \frac{12}{5}$. Thus a length, a width, and a diagonal form a right-angled triangle known as a Pythagorean triangle: $5^2+12^2 \div 13^2$.

The Egyptians knew and used this triangle, along with the $3^2 + 4^2 = 5^2$ triangle, to draw right angles.

Let us now divide the large side into twelve equal parts and the small side into 5, as indicated in Figure 34.

On side BC let us take Ba = 3 divisions, and on AD, Db = 3 divisions. Now let us join a and b, and we

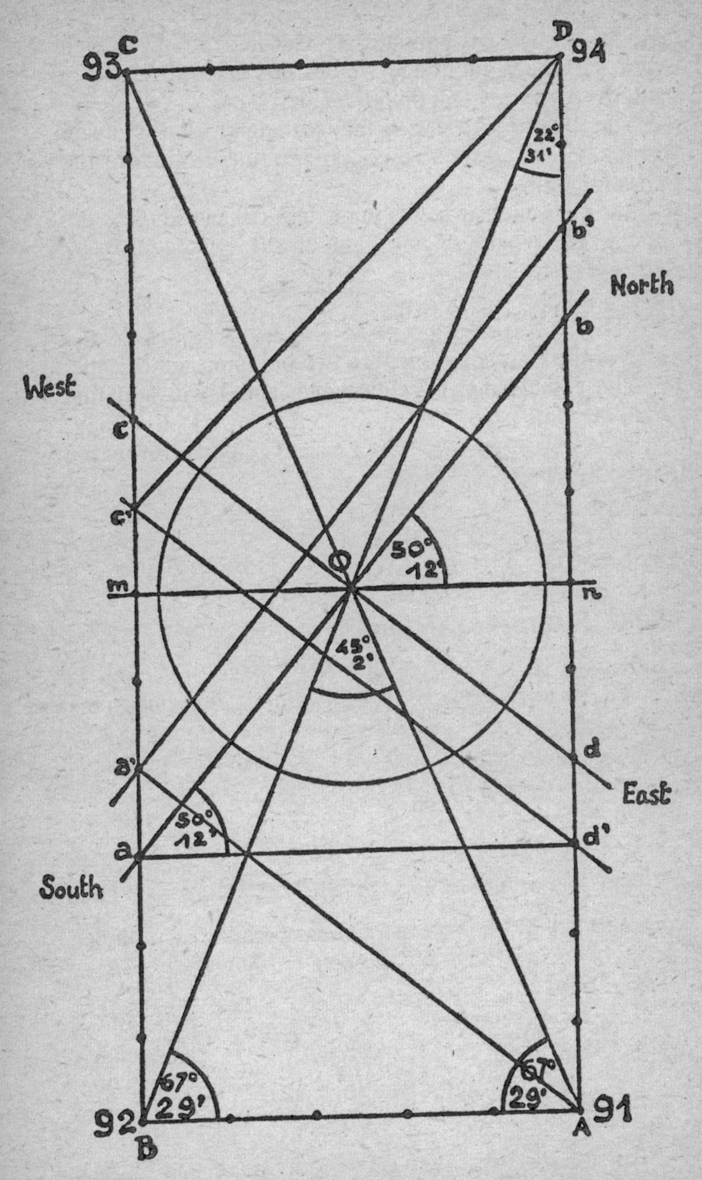
93
C
D
94
22°
31'
b'
North
b
West
c
c'
50°
12'
O
m
n
45°
2'
d
East
a'
50°
12'
d'
a
South
67°
29'
67°
29'
92
B
A
91

FIGURE 34

will have a meridian passing through the center of Stonehenge. In Figure 34 we see that this line forms an angle of 50°12′ with axis mn, which is the axis of the temple. This angle is equal, to within 20 minutes, to the azimuth of the axis of the structure with the meridian: 49°52′. A difference of 20 minutes in determining a meridian is not surprising. In the sixteenth century, Tycho Brahe made about the same error in orienting the Uraniborg observatory.

On side BC, let us take Cc = 4 divisions and, on AD, Ad = 4 divisions. By joining c to a, we obtain a line, also passing through the center of the structure, perpendicular to meridian ab and consequently marking the east-west direction.

These straight lines, marking the north-south and east-west directions, could not have been used for any kind of observation because they went through the monument, which precluded all visibility. But that drawback could easily have been eliminated. It would have been enough to draw parallel lines, for example, Dc′ or Aa′, passing outside the Sarsen Circle. Division of the sides into 12 and 5 equal parts would have made this simple to do.

Thus, a right-angled triangle with sides proportionate to 5, 12, and 13 has remarkable properties at the latitude of Stonehenge.

It also has a curious feature, which I have already pointed out in my book *La Civilisation des Mégalithes,* published in 1970.

Let us consider right-angled triangle ABD. Tangent BDA $= \frac{5}{12} = 0.4166$, which corresponds to an angle of 22°31′. Hence, in the same triangle, angle DBA is 90° − 22°31′ = 67°29′. If we now take triangle BOA, we have BOA = 180° − (67°29′ × 2) = 45°2′. It follows that in such a rectangle and in all similar rectangles, the diagonals intersect at 45°2′. This fact, which has so intrigued British students of Stonehenge, may simply be due to a geometrical coincidence.

In laying out the rectangle of the Four Stations, the builders may thus never have thought of seeing to it that the diagonals intersected at 45 degrees at the center of the figure. And it is hard to imagine why they should have wanted to do so. But what they do seem to have tried to achieve is a regular figure, a geometrically perfect rectangle with four precise right angles. The Egyptian 5-12-13 triangle gave them that possibility.

Appendix 3

Stonehenge Decoded

On October 26, 1963, an article that caused a sensation appeared in issue number 4904 of the famous British magazine *Nature*. It was entitled "Stonehenge Decoded." The author was Gerald S. Hawkins, an American astronomer at the Cambridge Observatory in Massachusetts. Ten years earlier he had worked at the experimental missile base at Larkhill, England, so he had often had occasion to visit Stonehenge and become interested in it. In his article he simply gave a brief summary of his work, but two years later he published a book with the same title in which he developed his conclusions at greater length. I can here give only a quick sketch of that attractively presented 200-page book.

When I first read *Stonehenge Decoded,* my reaction was one of great surprise. According to Hawkins, Stonehenge was a "Neolithic computer," a precision observatory used for predicting the positions of the risings and settings of the sun and moon, as well as eclipses! I assume he was convinced of these results beforehand, having probably been favorably impressed by Lockyer's work.

In about a hundred seconds, using an IBM 7090 computer, he discovered astonishing subtleties incorporated into Stonehenge. The computer gave the positions of the risings and settings of the sun and moon at the winter and summer solstices from 2001 to 1000 B.C., the period during which Stonehenge was built.

He thus had at his disposal a whole series of angles

and azimuths that he compared with those formed by the significant stones of Stonehenge, as shown in a plan. From these comparisons and measurements came the extraordinary results described above.

For sunrises and moonrises the main indicator was, of course, the Heel Stone, along with two other stones erected in the holes marked D and F in Figure 4. The Four Stations constituted other indicators.

Figure 35 is a drawing made on the basis of those in

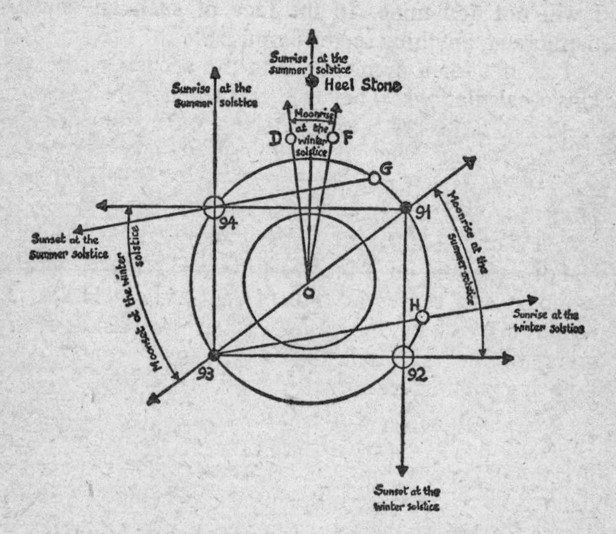

FIGURE 35—Sketch based on Gerald Hawkins' drawings.

which Hawkins indicates his main discoveries. Moonrise at the winter solstice, for example, oscillates within angle DOF, taking eighteen and a half years to cover that angle. Thus the moon sometimes rises over the Heel Stone, which is included in the angle, and when that happens, there is an eclipse. This is one of the directly observable results.

I will not describe the rather complicated system in which the circle of fifty-six Aubrey Holes functions as a protractor. Six index stones, three light-colored and three dark, were placed in holes separated by chosen intervals and were then advanced one hole each year, clockwise. When one of them reached a certain hole, the moon rose in a certain direction, and an eclipse took place.

It is easy to imagine the stir created by Hawkins's "revelations." They presupposed truly remarkable astronomical knowledge on the part of the builders. There was even talk of a "Neolithic Einstein!" Professional archaeologists were not sparing with their sarcasm, but I will not add mine. In the face of such an unusual monument, anything seems permissible.

I do not for a moment doubt the accuracy of Hawkins's calculations. They are mathematically rigorous, and his conclusions on the risings and settings of the sun and moon must be accepted without argument. But—there is a but—all this seems to me valid *in a plan*, that is, on paper. Transposed to Stonehenge itself, it is quite a different matter.

For example, on a plan, a little circle drawn with a compass can represent one of the Aubrey Holes, its center marked by the point of the compass, but try going to the site and finding the exact center of a hole dug with a deer antler!

What clearly shows that Hawkins's calculations are valid only in a plan is the part played by the center of the monument in possible observations. That center, defined by the intersection of the diagonals of the rectangle formed by the Four Stations, could no longer be found except in a very approximate way, after the sarsen structure had been erected. In any case it could not be located by the intersection of the diagonals, as I have explained earlier. No precise astronomical observation was possible from the center.

Hawkins's conclusions could have been drawn by others. There is no need of a computer to calculate the azimuth of a heavenly body at its rise. A slide rule will do the job quite well. Here is why many investigators have been hesitant: In such a monument, where close to a hundred stones are grouped in a limited area, it is possible to find all sorts of angles and directions that were not deliberately planned by the builders. At least as many could be discovered in a cathedral.

There are many more comments I could make on Hawkins's book, but I will stop here. Figure 35 is eloquent enough in itself for readers who have followed my descriptions.

There are so many people who, with the aid of a ruler, a compass, and a protractor, look for directions or geometrical figures in plans and maps! And they find them! But there is one thing that they must confess themselves unable to do: reproducing in another place, particularly a place with different latitude and longitude, what they have found in their plans.

That is why I say I am willing to believe in wondrous things associated with an old monument, provided they exist otherwise than on paper. At the same time, however, I want to avoid exaggerated skepticism and unreasonable criticism. There is one experiment that, I believe, would be convincing: laying out the design of another Stonehenge on the ground, far away from Salisbury Plain, using only means available to the builders of Stonehenge, that is, without trigonometric or astronomical tables and with almost nothing but wooden stakes and leather thongs.

When one studies old stones, analytical research is sometimes easy; attempts at synthesis are less so, as I know from experience. I remain convinced—and this will be my conclusion on these questions—that astronomy has not said its last word on the problems raised by Stonehenge. The heavenly bodies played a great part in the lives of people in past ages, who had nothing else to regulate their lives and work, and sometimes their beliefs, also. One simple question will illustrate my thought: Did the Heel Stone, which everyone sees as having indicated the point of sunrise at the summer solstice, mark the rise of the Pleiades, that ancient sailor's constellation mentioned by Diodorus Siculus? I am not able to solve that problem and the others, but sooner or later they will arise.